Family and Succession Law in Finland

Family and Succession Law in Finland

Tuulikki Mikkola

This book was originally published as a monograph in the International Encyclopaedia of Laws/Family and Succession Law.

Founding Editor: Roger Blanpain
General Editor: Frank Hendrickx
Volume Editor: Walter Pintens

Wolters Kluwer

Published by:
Kluwer Law International B.V.
PO Box 316
2400 AH Alphen aan den Rijn
The Netherlands
E-mail: international-sales@wolterskluwer.com
Website: lrus.wolterskluwer.com

Sold and distributed in North, Central and South America by:
Wolters Kluwer Legal & Regulatory U.S.
7201 McKinney Circle
Frederick, MD 21704
United States of America
Email: customer.service@wolterskluwer.com

Sold and distributed in all other countries by:
Air Business Subscriptions
Rockwood House
Haywards Heath
West Sussex
RH16 3DH
United Kingdom
Email: international-customerservice@wolterskluwer.com

Printed on acid-free paper

ISBN 978-94-035-0291-5

e-Book: ISBN 978-94-035-0180-2
web-PDF: ISBN 978-94-035-0254-0

Printed in the United Kingdom.

The Author

Tuulikki Mikkola graduated from the Faculty of Law at the University of Lapland in 1993 (LLM). After this, she studied at Nottingham University in 1994–1995. Mikkola started her research career as a member of a graduate school in 1995 in the Institute of International Economic Law (at University of Helsinki) and received her LL.D in the University of Lapland in 1999. In her dissertation Mikkola concentrated on a theory of comparative law and obstacles to obtaining correct information concerning foreign law, especially inheritance law.

At the moment Mikkola works as the professor of family law and private international law at the Faculty of Law, University of Turku. Before this, Mikkola has held various positions at law faculties in Helsinki University and the University of Lapland. She has also worked in research projects funded by the Academy of Finland. Mikkola has also worked as an advocate.

Mikkola's research interests include marital, family, and inheritance law and property law. Her areas of interest also include comparative law and more specifically English law. It has been her ambition to produce knowledge about how the method of comparative law can be tapped in researching substantive law. Examples of this are the monographs Trust (2003) and Fidusiaarivastuu (in English: Fiduciary Duty, 2006). As family and succession law have been the focus of Mikkola's work in substantive law, it is natural that issues in these areas has become her topics in the research she has pursued in private international law (*see*, e.g., monographs Kansainvälinen avioliitto- ja jäämistöoikeus (in English: International Marriage and Inheritance Law, 2004, 2009) and Kansainvälinen lapsioikeus (in English: International Child Law, 2012)).

The Author

Table of Contents

General Introduction

§1. General Background of the Country (Demographic Data)

1. Finland is a Nordic country. It covers an area of more than 338,000 sq. km and is situated on the northern fringe of Europe. Its neighboring countries are Sweden, Norway, and Russia. The Åland Islands form an autonomous and demilitarized province of Finland. Åland Islands are situated in the Baltic Sea, at the southern end of the Gulf of Bothnia between Finland and Sweden.

2. Finland has approximately 5.5 million inhabitants. Most of them live in the southern part of Finland; the population is concentrated in the capital city of Helsinki and the municipalities surrounding it. In general, Finland is a sparsely populated country with seventeen inhabitants per square kilometer.

3. The official languages are Finnish and Swedish.[1] Five percent of the population speaks Swedish as a first language. In addition, Sami is the first language of 2,000 people. Sami is spoken in the most northern part of Finland, Lapland.[2] Finland is ethnically quite homogeneous country. Some 70% of Finnish people belong to the Lutheran Church, therefore being the largest religious group. Thus, as a result of immigration (especially in recent years) the society has diversified[3] and it is expected that the other religious groups are about to grow in proportionate sizes.[4]

4. Finland was a part of Sweden until 1809 and part of the Russian Empire until 1917 and declared independence on December 6, 1917.

5. Finland is a sovereign republic, a welfare state with a strong tradition of the rule of law and has been a member of the European Union (EU) since 1995.

---

1. Language Act, s. 1 (423/2003, in English at: www.finlex.fi/fi/laki/kaannokset/2003/en20030423.pdf). Throughout this whole book, references to statutes are made with their respective numbers in the Statutes of Finland. The latter part of the number stipulates when the statute was published (usually also the year of the enactment). The number does not, thus, indicate the amendments made to the statute.
2. Sami people have had the right to use their own languages in courts and with public officials since 1991. *See also* revised Sámi Language Act of 2003, s. 1 (1086/2003, in English at: www.finlex.fi/fi/laki/kaannokset/2003/en20031086.pdf). *See also* the website of the Sami Parliament at: www.samediggi.fi/index.php?option=com_content&task=view&id=74&Itemid=167&lang=english.
3. Pauliina Raento & Kai Husso: Cultural Diversity in Finland. Fennia International Journal of Geography. Vol. 1-2/2001, pp. 151–164.
4. According to Statistics Finland, some 35,000 persons moved to Finland in 2016, which was approximately 20% more than one year earlier. Emigration also increased from the previous year, but clearly less than immigration. *See* Official Statistics of Finland: Migration, at: www.stat.fi/til/muutl/index_en.html. Statistics Finland collects the official statistics for Finland.

§2. Historical Background of Family and Succession Law

6. The Finnish legal system originated during the period of Swedish rule. Even when Finland was under Russian realm, Finland held an autonomous position covering, for instance, legislative powers. This meant that Swedish laws (the Swedish Civil Code) remained in force. As a consequence, the Swedish legal system has had an important and profound influence on the Finnish legal system. A few provisions of the Swedish Code of 1734 were in force in Finland even till the late 1980s.

7. Legislative co-operation with Sweden (and other Nordic countries) has traditionally been very important and fruitful. Many of those acts that were passed in the twentieth century —especially laws that were prepared during the first decades after Finland achieved independence - were prepared in co-operation with the other Nordic countries. Accordingly, there are identiable Nordic features in many important private law statutes.

8. The influence of the Nordic co-operation has covered also family and inheritance laws.[5] It should be noted, though, that in Finland (as in other Nordic countries) family and inheritance laws have been revised and amended on many occasions. For example, divorce system was radically streamlined in Finland in 1988. Legal developments have not always led to the same direction, and the legislative end results have been quite different even inside the Scandinavian borders. One example of this is the regulation of a widow's legal position.

9. During recent years Finnish legislator has faced new challenges as globalization has reached Finland. The development has affected naturally legislation in respect of cross-border cases, and comprehensive legislation concerning international families has been passed covering almost all areas of family and inheritance law.[6]

10. Over the years also the concept of a family has been changing. Cohabitees' legal rights in the dissolution of property are now recognized in written law (the Act on the Dissolution of the Household of Cohabiting Partners, 26/2011). Even earlier the Act on Registered Partnerships (950/2001) enabled same-sex couples to achieve a legal status that gave them the same rights and duties as spouses, unless otherwise specifically provided.

---

5. For the Nordic co-operation and the various forms it has taken over the years *see* Severin Blomstrand: Nordic Co-operation on Legislation in the Field of Private Law. Scandinavian Studies in Law. Vol. 39/2000, pp. 59–77. It should be noted, thus, that the co-operation has for various reasons (one of them is the EU) been on decline for some decades now, *see* Ulf Bernitz: What Is Scandinavian Law? Concept, Characteristics, Future. Scandinavian Studies in Law. Vol 50/2007, pp. 13–30. However, because of the many forms of communication that still takes place, Bernitz concludes "In summary, the legal similarity between the Nordic countries, when compared with Continental Europe and even more so the common law world, is still well-established and deep-seated." Accordingly, the forms of co-operation are changing and even though there is less room for direct legislative co-operation, the change of ideas certainly continues at a more general level. For instance, Nordic lawyers meet in inter-Nordic seminars etc. One can anticipate that this upholds certain legal unity also in the future.
6. Tuulikki Mikkola: The Risks and Opportunities of Foreign Connections in Marriages: the Proprietary Rights of Spouses. In: B. Atkin (ed.): The International Survey of Family Law, 2008 edition. Jordan Publishing 2008, pp. 77–106, p. 78.

11. A concept of marriage has renewed as well. Gender-neutral marriage has been legal in Finland since March 2017.

§3. Sources of Family and Succession Law

I. Introduction to the Sources of Law

12. Even though there are influences of continental law (especially German law) in all Nordic countries, the Nordic legal family has not been built on Roman law to the same extent as some other European legal systems.[7] This means, among other things, that Finnish law has not been codified in the proper sense of the term. Nonetheless, Finnish legal system can be described as a statutory law system as statutes, individual acts are the most important—and strongly binding—sources of law.[8] Under certain circumstances even a custom can be a strongly binding source of law. Pursuant the Code of Judicial Procedure (4/1734) Chapter 1 section 11: "A judge shall carefully examine the true purpose and grounds for the law and render judgment accordingly, and not as he or she pleases, against the law. In the absence of statutory law, the custom of the land, if not unreasonable, shall also be his or her guide in rendering judgment." Nonetheless, owing to detailed legislation, the importance of customary law is marginal throughout the areas of family and inheritance law.[9]

13. General legal principles have remained unwritten but despite this, the private law is seen as a systematic whole. Concepts and principles are its building blocks and their development is entrusted to legal science. Hence, doctrine and academic writings about the content of law are permitted sources and in practice normally consulted in

7. Ditlev Tamm: The Nordic Legal Tradition in European Context, In: Pia Letto-Vanamo, (ed): Nordisk identitet – Nordisk rätt i europeisk gemenskap. Institute for International Economic Law (KATTI), Helsinki University 1998, pp. 15–31, p. 15. From the perspective of comparative classifications, Nordic legal systems have traditionally been seen as belonging to the Romano-Germanic legal family. However, there are also dissenting opinions, stating that despite of the strong continental law impact and influence the Nordic legal families should be grouped as a family of their own. *See* Teemu Juutilainen: Finnish Private Law: Statutory System Without a Civil Code. In: J.C. Rivera (ed.): The Scope and Structure of Civil Codes. Springer Science + Business Media, Dordrecht 2013, pp. 155–180, p. 166.
8. The term statutes should be interpreted broadly. It covers both the Constitution Act and the acts of Parliament, as well as decrees and legal rules issued by lower-ranking authorities. For the nature of the legal order, sources of law and legal argumentation in Finland *see* Aulis Aarnio: Introduction. In J. Pöyhönen (ed.): An Introduction to Finnish Law. Kauppakaari, Helsinki 2002, pp. 1–20, pp. 12–13. Also Juha Raitio: The Source of Law – Doctrine and Reasoning in Finland, at: conference.ifla.org/ifla78, who writes that in court decisions one can find reflections of the legality principle. Emphasis lies more on the predictability than substantive justification. A comprehensive list of sources of law in Finland can also be found at: e-justice.europa.eu/content_member_state_law-6-fi-en.do?init=true&member=1.
9. Eva Gottberg: Study on Matrimonial Property Regimes and the Property of Unmarried Couples in Private International Law and Internal Law. National Report: Finland. Commission Européenne JAI/A3/2001/03, p. 1.

the interpretation of law. Even though references to doctrine are not openly included in the decisions of the Supreme Court, in the argumentation given by the lower courts these are occasionally, undisguisedly referred to. Permitted sources of law include also morality and factual arguments. These refer to substantive sources of law and their importance is based on the way the situation under consideration and the consequences of the different alternative decisions are regarded from the point of view of morality and justice.[10]

14. The legislative power is vested in the Parliament (in Finnish: *eduskunta*). The Parliament enacts laws but in its work it is strongly influenced by the preparatory phase. Therefore preparatory legislative work (*travaux preparatoires*) is often utilized in order to interpret "the legislator's meaning." The most important material in this respect is government proposals. They include detailed grounds for each chapter and section of the proposed enactment. Legislative drafts are considered as weakly binding sources of law.

15. Court decisions are also weakly binding sources of law. Still, in practice they carry much weight and are often referred to when interpreting and applying provisions of civil law. The most important are those cases decided in the Supreme Court and the Supreme Administrative Court. Cases these courts decide are called precedents.[11] Also cases handled by the courts of appeal can be significant sources of law, especially in cases where there are some alternative interpretations of the content of law but no Supreme Court decisions on the matter. This is usually the case with a fairly new provision of law. It should also be noted that as in order to have the case to be handled in the Supreme Court, the leave of appeal is required and therefore only a quite small number of cases is handled in the highest court. This system gives, in practice, weight to the decisions of the lower courts.[12]

16. Besides sources of law that originate on a domestic level, also those international obligations to which Finland is committed are strongly binding sources of law. The jurisprudence of the international operators that apply the obligations also has significance as a source of law.

10. Pekka Timonen: Sources of Law and Material on the Sources of Law. In J. Pöyhönen (ed.): An Introduction to Finnish Law. Kauppakaari, Helsinki 2002, pp. 21–30, p. 30.

11. Below the practice of the Supreme Court of Finland (in Finnish: *Korkein oikeus*; KKO) is referred to with the year and the publication number of the case. *See* the webpages of the Supreme Court, even in English at: www.korkeinoikeus.fi. Since 2017 the Supreme Court has published unofficial summaries of some of its precedents in English on its webpages. These precedents usually contain either issues from the standpoint of the law of the European union or of human rights or other international interests.

Until year 2015 precedents containing EU- or human rights related issues were translated into Swedish. This was due to co-operation between Nordic supreme courts. See English summaries at: http://korkeinoikeus.fi/en/index/ennakkopaatokset/shortsummariesofselectedprecedentsinenglish.html.

12. Aulis Aarnio: Precedent in Finland. In: N. MacCormick – R. Summers (eds.): Interpreting Precedents. A Comparative Study. Dartmouth & Ahsgate, 1997, pp. 65–102. For the overall role of precedents *see also* Pekka Timonen: Sources of Law and Material on the Sources of Law. In J. Pöyhönen (ed.): An Introduction to Finnish Law. Kauppakaari, Helsinki 2002, pp. 21–30, p. 29.

In addition, Finland is a member of the European Union, and has recognized the supremacy of EU law in the normative hierarchy over national law.

II. Constitution Act

17. The (new) Constitution Act (731/1999, in Finnish: *Perustuslaki*) has been in force since March 1, 2000. By this Constitution all previous documents with constitutional status (dating back to 1919–1928) were replaced.[13] The Constitution is the basis of all legislation and exercise of government powers. The constitutionality of government bills (proposal of new legislation or the amendment) is previewed in advance and this mainly takes place in the Parliament, and especially in its Constitutional Law Committee (*see* section 74 of the Constitution).[14] It is a body comprised of politicians, but in practice, it operates upon legal advice given by constitutional law experts, in most cases university professors.

18. There is no constitutional court in Finland. If a conflict between a provision in force and a basic right arises, the courts and authorities have a duty to follow a "Constitution-oriented interpretation approach." They should, in other words, interpret a certain provision of law in a way that it complies with the basic rights and if the application of an act would be in manifest conflict with the Constitution, the courts and authorities have to give preference to the Constitution, pursuant to the Constitution Act, section 106.[15]

19. The Constitution Act includes a comprehensive list of fundamental rights in its chapter II.[16] Some of these rights have more relevance than others in the area of family and succession law, and they lay down the value base of these legal areas. However, until quite recently, it was common to refer to basic rights in legislative work but they did not appear in judicial practice, concerning for instance matrimonial law. Nowadays the role of human and basic rights has changed in respect of family and inheritance law. They are now visible also in the argumentation of the courts as basic rights are used as maxims guiding the argumentation. This change has been most apparent in the area of child law.

20. In the Constitution Act, there is no specific provision in where the concept of family would be specifically included. Thus, there are certain other important provisions that affect the area of family and inheritance law. These include for instance the following provisions:

---

13. For the 1919 Constitution Act, independent Finland's first constitution, and its background *see* , e.g., the Constitution of Finland and Parliament's Rules of Procedure. Helsinki 2013 pp. 1–7, available at: www.eduskunta.fi/FI/tietoaeduskunnasta/julkaisut/Documents/ekj_3+2013.pdf.
14. Aulis Aarnio: Precedent in Finland. In: N. MacCormick – R. Summers (eds.): Interpreting Precedents. A Comparative Study. Dartmouth & Ahsgate, 1997, pp. 65–102, p. 66.
15. Juha Lavapuro – Tuomas Ojanen – Martin Scheinin: Rights-based Constitutionalism in Finland and the Development of Pluralist Constitutional Review. International Journal of Constitutional Law. Vol. 9/2011, pp. 505–531.
16. A thorough Finnish constitutional rights commentary is provided by i.e., Ilkka Saraviita: The Constitution of Finland. Kluwer Law International, The Haque 2005. *See also* Jaakko Nousiainen: The Constitution of Finland. The Ministry of Justice 2001 and Jaakko Husa: The Constitution of Finland: A Contextual Analysis. Hart Publishing 2011.

Section 6 - Equality

Everyone is equal before the law.

No one shall, without an acceptable reason, be treated differently from other persons on the ground of sex, age, origin, language, religion, conviction, opinion, health, disability or other reason that concerns his or her person.

Children shall be treated equally and as individuals and they shall be allowed to influence matters pertaining to themselves to a degree corresponding to their level of development.

Equality of the sexes is promoted in societal activity and working life, especially in the determination of pay and the other terms of employment, as provided in more detail by an Act.

Section 7 - The right to life, personal liberty and integrity

Everyone has the right to life, personal liberty, integrity and security.No one shall be sentenced to death, tortured or otherwise treated in a manner violating human dignity.

The personal integrity of the individual shall not be violated, nor shall anyone be deprived of liberty arbitrarily or without a reason prescribed by an Act. A penalty involving deprivation of liberty may be imposed only by a court of law. The lawfulness of other cases of deprivation of liberty may be submitted for review by a court of law. The rights of individuals deprived of their liberty shall be guaranteed by an Act.

The right of foreigners to enter Finland and to remain in the country is regulated by an Act. A foreigner shall not be deported, extradited or returned to another country, if in consequence he or she is in danger of a death sentence, torture or other treatment violating human dignity.

Section 10 - The right to privacy

Everyone's private life, honour and the sanctity of the home are guaranteed. More detailed provisions on the protection of personal data are laid down by an Act.

The secrecy of correspondence, telephony and other confidential communications is inviolable.

Measures encroaching on the sanctity of the home, and which are necessary for the purpose of guaranteeing basic rights and liberties or for the investigation of crime, may be laid down by an Act. In addition, provisions concerning limitations of the secrecy of communications which are necessary in the investigation of crimes that jeopardise the security of the individual or society or the sanctity of the home, at trials and security checks, as well as during the deprivation of liberty may be laid down by an Act.

Section 15 - Protection of property

The property of everyone is protected.

Provisions on the expropriation of property, for public needs and against full compensation, are laid down by an Act.

21. It should be stressed that the international human rights treaties hold a strong status within Finnish Law and also the Constitution Act includes references to internationally protected human rights. Case law of European courts is being viewed in detail and it therefore also affects the development of constitutionalism in Finland.[17] Moreover, the international treaties were a pool of inspiration when the chapter II of the Constitution Act was formulated. Therefore, when one is referring to the Constitution Act of Finland, it is justified to define it as a modern constitutional document of a European parliamentary democracy that operates within a European framework of rights protection.

17. Fundamental rights norms, whether based on constitutional rights provisions or on international human rights treaties, did not appear in court decisions until 1988. The turning point was Finland's signing of the European Convention of Human Rights in 1989, and the incorporation of its provisions into the domestic legal order in 1990. This has been said to represent one of the most important set of events in Finnish constitutional history. Juha Lavapuro – Tuomas Ojanen – Martin Scheinin: Rights-based Constitutionalism in Finland and the Development of Pluralist Constitutional Review. International Journal of Constitutional Law. Vol. 9/2011, pp. 505–531.

III. List of Main Legislation Concerning Family and Succession Law

22.

- the Marriage Act (234/1929);[18]
- the Code of Inheritance (40/1965);
- the Act on Registered Partnerships (950/2001);
- the Act on the Dissolution of the Household of Cohabiting Partners (26/2011);
- the Paternity Act (11/2015);
- the Adoption Act (22/2012);
- the Act on Assisted Fertility Treatments (1237/2006);
- the Act on Legal-Genetic Paternity Test (378/2005);
- the Child Custody and Rights of Access Act (361/1983);
- the Act on Enforcement of a Decision on Child Custody and Right of Access (619/1996);
- the Child Maintenance Act (704/1975);
- the Maintenance Support Act (580/2008);
- the Child Welfare Act (417/2007);
- The Guardianship Services Act (442/1999);
- the Act on the Arrangement of Guardianship Services Act (575/2008);
- the Continuing Power of Attorney Act (648/2007);
- the Names Act (694/1985).

IV. List of International Obligations and Treaties Concerning Family and Inheritance Law

23.

- the United Nations Covenant on the Rights of a Child November 20, 1989 (1130/1991);[19]
- the European Convention on Human Rights (439/1990);
- the Convention on the Protection of Children and Co-operation in Respect of Inter-country Adoption (497/1997);
- the Convention on the Civil Aspects of International Child Abduction (644/1994);
- the UN Convention on Consent to Marriage, Minimum Age for Marriage and Registration of Marriages December 10, 1962 (558/1964);
- the Convention on the Rights of Persons with Disabilities and its Optional Protocol (373/2015);
- the Hague on Jurisdiction, Applicable Law, Recognition, Enforcement and Co-operation in Respect of Parental Responsibility and Measures for the Protection of Children (8/2011);
- the Hague Convention on the International Protection of Adults (SopS 10/2011).

18. Note that the list is not supposed to be exhaustive.
19. Note that the list is not supposed to be exhaustive.

24. One should also note the importance of Nordic co-operation in the area of private international law. The co-operation has led to important conventions, such as:

- The Convention on the Recognition and Enforcement of Civil Judgments (56/1977).
- The Nordic Convention on Succession (21/1935).
- The Nordic Convention on Marriage (20/1931).

25. With the rise in number in cross-border family and inheritance matters and problems created by them between Member States of the European Union, EU has passed regulations to settle some of these issues. These include, e.g., the following:

- Regulation (EC) No 2201/2003 concerning jurisdiction and the recognition and enforcement of judgments in matrimonial matters and the matters of parental responsibility, repealing Regulation (EC) No 1347/2000.
- Regulation (EU) No 4/2009 on jurisdiction, applicable law, recognition and enforcement of decisions and cooperation in matters relating to maintenance obligations.
- Regulation (EU) No 650/2012 on jurisdiction, applicable law, recognition and enforcement of decisions and acceptance and enforcement of authentic instruments in matters of succession and on the creation of a European Certificate of Succession.

26. Regulation (EU) No 1103/2016 on jurisdiction, applicable law, and the recognition and enforcement of decisions in matters of matrimonial property regimes and Regulation (EU) No 1104/2016 on jurisdiction, applicable law, and the recognition and enforcement of decisions in matters of the property consequences of registered partnerships will apply from the January 29, 2019.

Rome III Regulation (EU) No 1259/2010 implementing enhanced cooperation in the area of the law applicable to divorce and legal separation is not applied in Finland.

§4. THE COURTS ADMINISTERING FAMILY AND SUCCESSION LAW

27. Finnish courts are divided into two main branches. General courts deal with civil law and criminal law matters. Administrative courts handle administrative litigation cases. The division between general and administrative courts dates back to 1919. The Supreme Court and the Supreme Administrative Court are independent in relation to each other and have no jurisdiction over one another.

28. There is no constitutional court in Finland.

29. The starting point is that family and inheritance law belongs to the jurisdiction of the general courts, covering issues of, for instance, paternity, divorce, and maintenance. Some cases, however, relating to family and inheritance law are handled in the administrative courts if they involve a public law dimension. Examples are child protection issues, cases of taxation and name changes.[20]

30. The general civil court system includes three levels: courts of a first instance (district courts), courts of appeal, and the Supreme Court. If a party is not satisfied with the decision of a district court, it is possible to appeal to a court of appeal. The consideration of most appeals, thus, requires leave for continued consideration granted by the court of appeal.[21] The function of the Supreme Court is to create precedents and to ensure uniformity in the administration of justice by the lower courts. The leave to appeal is granted by the Supreme Court itself only in cases where, according to the Code of Judicial Procedure (4/1734), Chapter 30, section 3 "it is important for the application of the law in similar situations or there is a reason to correct a mistake or defect, or there is another weighty reason."[22] The Supreme Court decides approximately 100–150 cases per year and they are published at the website of the Supreme Court and they are also available in a specific database called FINLEX.

31. Finlex (www.finlex.fi) is a legal databank in which legal information is organized into several databases. In order to browse Finlex, there is no need for subscription and its browsing is free of charge. Legislative information can be found at six databases, including, for instance, the database of translations of Finnish acts and decrees. Case law is published in separate databases. These include, e.g., the precedents given by the Supreme Court and the courts of appeal. There is also a database including information on references to case law in legal literature. In addition, Finlex includes a database for international treaties.

32. There are also other databases, besides Finlex, which include legislative information, information on case law, and legal literature. These databases usually require subscription and are commercial by nature.[23] On webpages of different authorities are also a list of decisions available free of charge.[24] An example is the Ombudsman and Deputy-Ombudsmen whose decisions are partly published on their websites.[25]

33. Civil disputes may also be handled in a mediation (in Finnish: *sovittelu*) procedure. A mediation process aims at an amicable end-result where the parties themselves find a solution to their conflict (Act on Mediation in Civil Matters and Confirmation of Settlements in the General Courts, 394/2011). Mediation is voluntary

20. Sanna Koulu: Towards a Negotiatory Ideal? Contractualisation of Family Law in Finland. In: F. Swennen (ed.): Contractualization of Family Law – Global Perspectives. Springer International Publishing 2015, pp. 193–216, p. 194.

21. In certain cases, however, leave is not needed. For these cases and the requirements for granting leave in other cases, *see* https://oikeus.fi/tuomioistuimet/karajaoikeudet/en/index/Appeals/jatkokasittelylupa.html.

22. *See* the webpages of the Supreme Court, at: korkeinoikeus.fi/en/index/appeal.html. Also Aulis Aarnio: Precedent in Finland. In: N. MacCormick – R. Summers (eds.): Interpreting Precedents. A Comparative Study. Dartmouth & Ahsgate, 1997, pp. 65–102.

23. For example Edilex, at: www.edilex.fi and Suomen Laki, at: suomenlaki.almatalent.fi.

24. *See* , for instance, the webpages of the Data Protection Ombudsman, at: www.tietosuoja.fi. There are listed decisions concerning the application of legislation and implementation of the rights of data subjects (in Finnish).

25. Decisions of the Ombudsman and Deputy-Ombudsmen are partly published on the website of the Ombudsman, at: www.oikeusasiamies.fi in Finnish but there are press releases of some of the decisions also in English.

and it is managed either by a judge (court mediation) or by a person who provides mediation services. Various types of civil law cases can be subject to mediation. For instance, disputes related to child law, such as child custody, right of access, and child maintenance may be settled in a mediation process.[26]

26. For mediation process and its requirements *see* Kaijus Ervasti: Court Mediation in Finland. National Research Institute of Legal Policy. Research Report No 256 Helsinki 2011, available at: helda.helsinki.fi/bitstream/.../summary_ti-sovittelu.pdf?...2. A brochure on court-annexed judicial mediation is available on the webpages of Judicial Administration, at: oikeus.fi/tuomioistuimet/karajaoikeudet/en/index/riita-asiat_1/riidansovittelu/tuomioistuimenulkopuolinensovittelu.htm. *See also* webpages for the Finnish Forum for Mediation, at: www.ssf-ffm.com/english/index.php.

Part I. Persons

Chapter 1. The Status of a Person

§1. Definition of a Person

34. Persons are either natural or legal and subjects of law (in Finnish: *oikeussubjekti*). This involves either the holding of rights and bearing of duties or the "legal capacity" to hold rights and bear duties. Legal capacity has been described as a basic right in a democracy and a cornerstone of a well-functioning legal order.

35. Person's ability to hold rights and bear duties begins at birth. The only requirement for it is that a person is born alive. A child is considered to be born alive if there are some certain signs of life. Life expectancy does not matter.[27] Under the provisions of the Code of Inheritance the interests of an unborn child are recognized as Chapter 1 section 1 states in a following way:

> Only a person who was alive at the time of the death of the decedent may inherit; however, a child conceived before the said time and born alive shall inherit.

36. A natural person is the subject of rights and addressee of duties until he/she dies. A person is declared dead after a complete loss of brain functions. The detailed guidelines concerning the determination of death can be found in the decree given by the Ministry of Social Affairs and Health (27/2004).

37. Time of death is related to the question of organ donation. Provisions on organ transplantation are specified in the Act of the Medical Use of Human Organs and Tissues (101/2001).[28] It covers the preconditions for organ donation and the donor's consent. According to the act the preconditions include for instance that the certification of death must be impartial and carried out exclusively on medical grounds. The doctors that certify the death of a person cannot be involved in organ transplantation.[29]

27. Even though an unborn child is not able to hold rights or bear duties, the fetus is given protection by provisions of the Act on Termination of Pregnancy (239/1970).
28. An English translation is available at: www.finlex.fi/fi/laki/kaannokset/2001/en20010101.pdf.
29. Organ transplantation is part of specialized medical care. Therefore the general medical legislation also applies, including the Health Care Act (1326/2010), the Act on the Status and Rights of Patients (785/1992), the Act on Specialized Medical Care (1062/1989) and the Act on Health Care Professionals (559/1994).

38. In some cases the whereabouts of a person are unknown and medical declaration of a death is not possible. Thus, missing persons can be declared dead through a judicial decision (the Act on Declaration of Death, 127/2005). A petition for a declaration can be submitted immediately after a person has been gone missing if at the time of the disappearance the person was in an accident causing immediate mortal danger. A petition can also be submitted after a waiting period. The length of a waiting time varies from one to five years depending on the circumstances. The court decides if a person is declared dead. If so, the decision is entered into the Population Information System.

39. Even though a person does not hold rights or bear duties after his/her death, some personal rights continue to be in force. A deceased's dignity is protected in numerous ways. For instance, according to the Act on Burial Service (457/2003) the wishes of the deceased should be honored as far as possible in the burial. In addition, if somebody dishonors the memory of the deceased, by spreading, for instance, a false information, in a way that it causes suffering to a person to whom the deceased was particularly close, the person spreading the false information can be sentenced for defamation (the Criminal Code (39/1889), Chapter 24, section 9(2)).[30]

Also the right to privacy survives death to some extent. The duration of this right is limited, though.[31]

§2. Capacity

I. General

40. When a person is able to make decisions that affect his/her rights and duties, he/she is said to have a capacity to enter into legal transactions. A capacity of a minor is limited and it does not begin in full until a person reaches majority, in other words turns 18 years. After this a person has a capacity to make binding agreements, enter into contracts, make gifts etc. There are exceptions to this rule, though, if a person is unable to take care of his/her responsibilities for instance due to illness.

When the law hinders or limits a person from engaging in certain specified activities, any agreements such person has contracted are either voidable or void for incapacity. Sometimes such legal incapacity is referred to as *incompetence*.

II. Minors

41. When a person is under 18 years of age, he/she is competent to enter into transactions if they are—in view of the circumstances—usual and of little significance

30. An English translation of the Criminal Code is available at: www.finlex.fi/fi/laki/kaannokset/1889/en18890039.pdf.
31. For the protection of privacy, *see* the English webpages of Data Protection Ombudsman, available at: www.tietosuoja.fi/en/index.html.

(the Guardianship Services Act (442/1999), section 24).[32] For instance, if an infant person enters a contract concerning necessities, the contract is valid and enforceable.

In general, if a person is under 18 years of age, he/she needs a legal representation in order to enter into binding legal transactions. Each child has a guardian whose duties include looking after the child's financial interests. The custodians of a minor are his/her guardians unless the court appoints another person for the task. Therefore the main rule is that custodians of a minor are also responsible for the administration of the child's property as guardians of the child (the Guardianship Services Act, section 4). Also a special guardian may be appointed in order to administer the child's property.

42. The Child Custody and the Right of Access Act (361/1983), section 4, provides that the custodian should discuss matters relating to the child with the child, and in this respect to give regard to the child's age and maturity. A custodian should, in other words, give due and proper consideration to the opinions of the child. There are no legally set age limits concerning the custodian's duty to take notice of the opinions of the child. It is obvious, though, that the child's right to take part in decisions concerning his/her own affairs naturally expands as the child grows older.

The guardian must obtain the permission of the Local Registry Office before entering into certain important transactions concerning the property of the minor. A permission is needed, e.g., for the selling or buying of real estate and the pledging of property as collateral for a debt. The guardian has no right to donate the minor's property. The guardian cannot represent the child in a transaction where the guardian him/herself is a party. In these cases an alternate guardian is required for such transactions (*see* the Guardianship Services Act, sections 32, 34).

43. A person who is over 15 years of age may enter into, terminate, or cancel an employment contract. Thus, the guardian may intervene and cancel the employment contract but only if the contract is harmful to the minor's education, development, or health. A minor also has a right to administer his/her own earnings. Again, exceptionally the guardian has the right to take this property into his or her administration if the earnings are otherwise administered in a way that is obviously contrary to the best interests of the minor (the Guardianship Services Act, section 25).

A person who has reached the age of 18 years may dispose of his or her property mortis causa by a will (the Code of Inheritance, Chapter 9, section 1). A minor person may also make a will, if he/she is or has been married. A person who is 15 years of age may make a will with regard to property that he/she is entitled to administer him/herself.

44. A minor child has the right to decide upon the way he/she is medically treated. It is, thus, required that the child has reached an age and maturity which allow him/her to perceive the meaning of the treatment and its consequences (the Act on the

32. An English translation available at: www.finlex.fi/en/laki/kaannokset/1999/en19990442.

Status and Rights of Patients (785/1992), section 7).[33] If this is not the case, the custodian or other legal representative of the child take part in the decisions concerning how the child is medically treated.

45. A custodian represents the child in matters relating to person of the child, unless otherwise provided by law (the Child Custody and the Right of Access Act, section 4). It is noteworthy, though, that according to procedural law, usually a child who has reached the age 15 has the right to self-representation in cases relating to his/her person. However, the custodian has a parallel right to represent the minor in these cases. The rule applies to civil and criminal proceedings and also to administrative proceedings (the Code of Judicial Procedure (4/1734), Chapter 12, sections 1–2;[34] the Act on Administrative Procedure (434/2003), section 14(3)).[35] In care proceedings, a child has a right to obtain information, and to present a view on the case in a manner that is appropriate in view of his/her age and level of development. A child whose welfare case is in question has certain procedural rights (separately or parallel with their custodians), such as the right to appeal if he/she is 12 or more years old (the Act on Child Welfare (417/2007), sections 5, 89).[36]

46. There are other examples where an opinion of the child should directly influence a decision-making process of an authority. The child's consent is needed if a petition is submitted for changing the child's first or family name and the child is at least 12 years old. Before reaching the age of 12 a child can prevent the change of his/her name, if he/she demonstrates such maturity that his/her will should be taken into consideration (the Names Act (694/1985), section 33).[37] In addition, a child that is 12 years of age or older can prevent his/her adoption. Even if the child is younger, his/her will can also be taken into consideration (the Adoption Act (22/2012), section 10).[38] Furthermore, a child may prevent the enforcement of a decision concerning custody or right of access (the Act of the Enforcement of a Decision on Child Custody and Right of Access (619/1996), section 2).[39]

---

33. In the Act on the Status and Rights of Patients the rights of a patient are divided into three categories: the right to good health care, the right to be informed, and the right to self-determination and participation. An English translation of the Act can be found at: www.finlex.fi/en/laki/kaannokset/1992/en19920785. The Act on the Status and Rights of Patients has been described to be the first act in the world that comprehensively regulates the rights of the patients. *See* , i.e., Lars Fallberg – Mervi Kattelus: The Ombudsman in Finland. In: S.Mackenney – L.Fallberg (eds.): Protecting Patients' Rights? A Comparative Study of the Ombudsman in Healthcare. Radcliffe Publishing Ltd 2004 pp. 25–32, p. 25. Also Lars Fallberg: Patients Rights in the Nordic Countries. European Journal of Health Law. Vol. 7/2000 pp. 123–143.
34. In English at: www.finlex.fi/fi/laki/kaannokset/1734/en17340004.pdf.
35. In English at: www.finlex.fi/fi/laki/kaannokset/2003/en20030434.pdf.
36. Mirja Satka - Timo Harrikari: The Present Finnish Formation of Child Welfare and History. British Journal of Social Work, doi:10.1093/bjsw/bcn037. Also Tarja Pösö – Raija Huhtanen: Removals of Children in Finland. In: K. Burns – T.Pösö – M. Skivenes (eds.): Child Welfare Removals by the State. Oxford University Press 2017, pp. 18–39, pp. 22–23.
37. In English available at: www.finlex.fi/en/laki/kaannokset/1985/en19850694.
38. For an English translation *see* www.finlex.fi/fi/laki/kaannokset/2012/en20120022.pdf.
39. Eira Kuisma: Comparative study on enforcement procedures of family rights. National Report Finland. JLS/C4/2005/06, T.M.C. Asser Instituut, p. 6.

III. Responsibility for Delict

47. The statute applicable to liability in damages is the Tort Liability Act (412/1974).[40] The act applies both to tort liability and the amount of damages. The act does not apply to contractual liability or to liability provided in another act (the Tort Liability Act, section 1). The act applies the principle of full compensation.

48. There are no set age limits as when a person has a responsibility for damages he/she has caused to another person. A guardian is not automatically responsible for actions taken by the child, if there has not been gross-negligence on part of the guardian in respect of his/her responsibility of looking after the child. Accordingly, children have no defense of minority and in practice even a child under 10 years of age has been held responsible for the damages he/she has caused.[41] However, in case of minors the amount of damages can be reduced if equitable grounds for this exist. In this respect the Tort Liability Act is based on consideration of circumstances as Chapter 2, section 2, states that if the injury or damage has been caused by a person under 18 years of age, he/she shall be liable for damages to an amount that is deemed reasonable in view of his/her age and maturity, the nature of the act, the financial status of the person causing the injury or damage and the person suffering the same, and the other circumstances.

49. A person is normally liable for damages in full after reaching the age of 18. There are, thus, certain limited exceptions to this rule. Namely, an insane, retarded or mentally disturbed person is liable for damages for injury or damage that he/she has caused to an amount that is deemed reasonable in view of his/her condition, the nature of the act, the financial status of the person causing the injury or damage and the person suffering the same, and the other circumstances. However, a temporary, self-inflicted mental disturbance of the person causing the injury or damage is not in itself deemed a reason for reducing his/her liability for damages (the Tort Liability Act, Chapter 2, section 3).

IV. Criminal Liability

50. The basic statute in criminal law is the Penal Code of 1889 (39/1889).[42] Under the Code a person has a criminal liability after reaching the age of 15 (the Penal Code, Chapter 3, section 4). Before that age, the act does not come to trial. However, the Child Welfare Act contains provisions concerning minors who have committed crimes under 15 years of age. The social welfare authorities and the police try together

---

40. In English at: www.finlex.fi/fi/laki/kaannokset/1974/en19740412.
41. In the Supreme Court Case KKO 1991:73 damages were awarded against a girl who was fifteen at the time the damage occurred. She had been hanging out with her boyfriend (also fifteen year at the time) who set fire to rubbish bins next to a building and as a result the whole building caught fire, as well. The court held that a girl had deliberately encouraged her boyfriend in his actions and therefore she was also held responsible for the damages caused.
42. An English translation can be found at: www.finlex.fi/fi/laki/kaannokset/1889/en18890039?search%5Btype%5D=pika&search%5Bpika%5D=rikoslaki.

to give such support that such person learns to live a life without committing criminal acts. Under the child welfare system, the best interests of the child prevail.

51. When an offender is between 15 and 17 years of age, he/she is subject both to the criminal justice system and to the child welfare system. Again at this stage, all interventions under the child welfare system are supportive.[43] In the court the difference in the sentencing of young and adult offenders lies in the reduction rule that is applied to the sentence of the former (for a mitigated scale of punishment *see* the Penal Code, Chapter 6, section 8). In addition, if a perpetrator was under 18 years of age at the time of the offense, he/she cannot be sentenced to unconditional imprisonment without weighty reasons.[44]

If an offender is still not yet 21 years, he/she is called a young offender. There are no special rules applicable to their sentencing, except the one stating that young offenders are released on parole earlier than adult offenders.

52. Mediation can be used in addition or as an alternative to judicial proceedings, and can be used also in cases where a child is an offender. Mediation is defined in the Act on Conciliation in Criminal and Certain Civil Cases (1015/2005), section 1, in the following way: "conciliation in criminal cases (*conciliation*) means a non-chargeable service in which a crime suspect and the victim of that crime are provided the opportunity to meet confidentially through an independent conciliator, to discuss the mental and material harm caused to the victim by the crime and, on their own initiative, to agree on measures to redress the harm." The act lays down requirements for the mediation, including that the parties agree to the mediation. In case a perpetrator is under-aged, his/her legal representatives (such as custodians) have to agree to the mediation (section 2 of the Act on Conciliation in Criminal and Certain Civil Cases).[45] If the parties reach an agreement, the mediator draws up a document on it. In cases of lesser crimes, the agreement may result in discontinuance of the criminal proceedings. The agreement may also at a later stage lead to non-prosecution, waiving of sentence or to a more lenient punishment.[46]

V. Majors

53. The starting point is that a person has a full legal competency after reaching majority, at the age of 18 years. However, if a person, due to illness or some comparable reason, is unable to take care or look after of his/her interests or personal matters, a

43. Tapio Lappi-Seppälä: Alternatives to Custody for Young Offenders. National Report on Juvenile Justice Trends: Finland. International Juvenile Justice Observatory p. 2, at: www.oijj.org/sites/default/files/baaf_finland1.pdf. *See also* Tapio Lappi-seppälä: Finland: A Model of Tolerance? In: John Muncie - Barry Goldson (eds.): Comparative Youth Justice 2006, pp. 177–195.

44. Matti Marttunen: The Basis of Finnish Juvenile Criminal Justice. Revue internationale de droit penal. Vol. 75/2004, pp. 315–335, at: www.cairn.info/revue-internationale-de-droit-penal-2004-1-page-315.htm.

45. Ilona Nieminen: Study on Children's Involvement in Judicial Proceedings. Contextual Overview for the Criminal Justice Phase: Finland. European Union, 2014 pp. 13–19.

46. *See* more closely, for instance oikeus.fi/syyttaja/en/index/asioiminensyyttajankanssa/rikosasioidensovittelu.html.

legal representative (a guardian, in Finnish: *edunvalvoja*) is appointed to make decisions on behalf of a person (a ward).[47] The primary task of the guardian is to take care of all financial affairs of the ward.[48] In addition to financial affairs, the guardian must ensure that the ward is suitably treated and receives care and rehabilitation.

54. Normally, a ward's own competency is not restricted by the appointment of a guardian. The basic principle of the Guardianship Services Act is to safeguard the interests of the ward in a way that his/her own competency is protected as far as possible. Therefore the starting point is to appoint a supportive guardian in order to help a person to administer his/her property. In this option the appointment of a guardian does not disqualify the person from self- managing his/her financial affairs or entering into transactions (the Guardianship Services Act, section 14).[49] If the ward is, thus, in practice incapable of entering the transaction, it may be declared null and void in a court.

55. It is also possible to restrict a competency of a person, but not more than what is necessary in order to safeguard the ward's interests and to protect him/her. The requirement for the restriction is that a person is unable to take care of his/her financial affairs and his/her property, and because of this the livelihood or other important interests are thereby at risk and the appointment of a guardian is not alone considered sufficient to safeguard his/her interests. There are three options what a court can do in restricting competency of a person. It can order that:

(1) a person may enter into given transactions or administer given property only in conjunction with the guardian;
(2) a person is not competent to enter into given transactions or to administer given property; or
(3) a person is declared incompetent.

56. The third option is the last resort (the Guardianship Services Act, section 18).

In practice, a court tailors the restrictions to meet the individual circumstances and defines, for instance, certain specific transactions that a ward cannot enter. Declaring a person generally incompetent is an option very seldom used.[50]

47. An appointment of a guardian can be made by a Local Registry Office or a district court, *see* the Guardianship Services Act, ss. 10–12. A person close to the client may be named for the task of a guardian. Also a public guardian can be appointed for instance when the Local Registry Office has not found any close relative or other person fit for the task.
48. A guardian may also be appointed only for the performance of an individual task, such as the sale of real estate on behalf of the client (the Guardianship Services Act, s. 8). For an English translation of the Act, *see* www.finlex.fi/en/laki/kaannokset/1999/en19990442.pdf.
49. Markku Helin: Finland. In: R. Frimston – A. Ruck Keene – C. Van Overdijk – A.D. Ward (eds.): The International Protection of Adults. Oxford University Press 2015, pp. 356–363, p. 358: "The guiding principles on the appointment of a legal representative derive from the concepts of subsidiarity and proportionality. Thus, legal representatives may not be given powers in excess of what is necessary to carry out their specific functions."
50. Markku Helin: Finland. In: R. Frimston – A. Ruck Keene – C. Van Overdijk – A.D. Ward (eds.): The International Protection of Adults. Oxford University Press 2015, pp. 356–363, p. 359.

If a person is, however, declared incompetent, he/she cannot administer his/her property or enter into transactions—except the ones that are in view of the circumstances usual and of little significance. It is noteworthy, though, that even though a person who has been declared incompetent may self-decide on personal matters, if he/she is able to understand the significance of the matter (the Guardianship Services Act, section 23). In addition, the guardian is never competent to give a consent to a marriage or an adoption on the behalf of the ward, nor to acknowledge paternity, consent to an acknowledgement of paternity, make or revoke a will or represent the ward in other matters of a comparably personal and individual nature (the Guardianship Services Act, section 29).

57. The guardian has to act prudently on behalf of the ward and take care of the property so that it can be used, i.e., for the satisfaction of the ward's personal needs. In order to safeguard ward's interests, a guardian is monitored by a guardianship authority (the Local Registry Office, the Guardianship Services Act, section 46). A guardian is responsible for keeping books and accounts during the administration. After the appointment of the guardian, an inventory and management plan of the assets and liabilities of the ward have to be submitted to the Registry Office, and the guardian is also obliged to submit regular (usually annual) accounts to the Registry Office.[51]

A guardian is not free to enter any transaction on behalf of the ward that he/she sees necessary. Instead, a guardian must obtain the permission of the Registry Office before entering into certain transactions. A permission is needed, e.g., for the selling or buying of real estate, raising a lien on the property, taking out of some other loan than a state-guaranteed student loan etc. (the Guardianship Services Act, section 34). The guardian is not ever empowered to donate the property of the ward and such permission is not even obtainable from the guardianship authority.

The ward's interests are also protected by a rule that a guardian cannot represent the ward in a transaction where the guardian him/herself—or a person close to the guardian—is counterparty (the Guardianship Services Act, section 32). For entering such transaction a nomination of a substitute guardian is required.

58. It is also possible that a person (grantor) issues a continuing power of attorney (in Finnish: *edunvalvontavaltuutus*), intended to be applied in case grantor's functional capacity is later decreased to such extent that he/she is not able to self-administer his/her property and enter any valid transactions. By issuing the document, it is possible to nominate such a person as the grantor trusts and is fit to act on behalf of him/her. A grantor is also free to define the scope of the powers as he/she sees necessary.[52] The authorization may be general or limited to certain tasks/cover specific property specified in the document. The document may also cover personal and health care matters.[53]

51. For the property management *see* the Guardianship Services Act, ss. 37–41.

52. It is even possible to give powers to donate the grantor's property in the authorization but this must be expressly provided in the deed. Markku Helin: Finland. In: R. Frimston – A. Ruck Keene – C. Van Overdijk – A.D. Ward (eds.): The International Protection of Adults. Oxford University Press 2015, pp. 356–363, p. 360.

53. A brochure of a continuing power of attorney can be found at (in English): oikeus.fi/en/index/esitteet/edunvalvontavaltuutus/mitenedunvalvontavaltuutustehdaan.html. The Act on Continuing Powers of Attorney (648/2007) can be found at: www.finlex.fi/fi/laki/ajantasa/2007/20070648 but only in Finnish and Swedish.

§3. Absentees

59. A court has to appoint a guardian if a deceased left an inheritance and a person who is a legal heir or a beneficiary under a will is absent and his or her whereabouts are unknown (the Guardianship Services Act, section 10). A guardian manages the property on behalf of the absentee. If a guardian is needed to look after the interests of an absent person, those who are able to file a petition are listed in the Guardianship Services Act, section 72. Among those are the administrator, other caretaker, distributor, or shareholder in the estate and under certain circumstances also a person whose right or interest is affected by the matter.

Chapter 2. Registration of Civil Status

§1. The Registrar

60. The Population Information System (in Finnish: *väestötietojärjestelmä*) is maintained by the Population Register Centre and Local Registry Offices (in Finnish: *maistraatti*). Registry Offices are local state administrative authorities and the operational area of each covers one or more jurisdictional districts. The purpose is to ensure that services are widely enough available to the public.

Everyone residing in Finland for periods exceeding three months is registered with the Population Information System. Such information of a person as name, date of birth, nationality, family relationships, and address is entered into the system. In addition to these, the system also includes data on real estate, buildings and apartments. The information system has been defined to serve modern society's varied needs for information.[54] The information collected is confidentially used for purposes like taxation and judicial administration, and also for statistical purposes.

61. If a person is registered in the Population Information System, he/she may receive a personal identity number/code (in Finnish: *henkilötunnus*), which is an identification more specific than a name. It is needed often and in many situations of everyday life—such as renting a flat or in health care. A child born in Finland is issued with a personal identity code automatically once the hospital has reported the child's birth to the Population Information System. A Finnish citizen born outside Finland can obtain a personal identity code by presenting his/her birth certificate at a Local Registry Office. Furthermore, a foreign national residing in Finland permanently—or if his/her stay exceeds one year—may also be issued with a personal identity code.[55]

§2. Registers and Certificates

62. The Local Registry Offices maintain the Population Information System and their local information services. They serve as the guardianship authority, as well. Other services offered by the Local Registry Offices include notary public services, the investigation of impediments to marriage and performances of civil marriages. They also handle matters concerning name changes and the confirmation of the list of parties to estate inventories.

It is noteworthy that the Local Registry Offices have also provided consumer advisory services since 2009.

54. *See* the webpages of Population Register Centre at: vrk.fi/en/check-your-registered-data-. The basic acts in relation to collecting, storing and utilizing the data are the Population Information Act (661/2009) and the Personal Data Act (523/1999, in English at: www.finlex.fi/en/laki/kaannokset/1999/en19990523.pdf).

55. The identity number is personal. It does not change during one's lifetime. There are, however, certain exceptions to this rule for instance in cases of witness protection etc.

European Certificates of Succession are granted by the Local Registry Office of Uusimaa.[56]

56. For more information concerning tasks of Local Registry Offices, *see* www.maistraatti.fi/en/.

Chapter 3. Protection of Personal Data

63. The right to privacy is listed as a fundamental right in the Constitution Act, section 10.[57] The more detailed provisions on the processing of personal data are included in the Personal Data Act (523/1999) which implemented the EU Directive on Data Protection (95/46/EC).[58]

The first section of the Personal Data Act states the objectives of the act in a following way: "to implement, in the processing of personal data, the protection of private life and the other basic rights which safeguard the right to privacy, as well as to promote the development of and compliance with good processing practice." Everybody has a right to privacy and it cannot be restricted without an explicit basis provided by the Personal Data Act.

64. As mentioned earlier, the protection of natural persons in relation to the processing of personal data is a fundamental right. Accordingly, the basic rights and freedom of individuals to privacy and self-determination are strongly emphasized in the processing of personal data. To this end, one of the most important provisions of Personal Data Act gives a person a right of access; in other words, right to know what information of him/her is included in the personal data register (the Personal Data Act section 26). If it is incorrect, superseded, misleading etc., the registrar is under an obligation to alter the information.

It should be noted, though, that the Regulation on data protection entered into force in May 2016, and it is applicable from May 25, 2018.[59] The regulation repeals the earlier directive and is directly applicable in the Member States and therefore no need for additional domestic legislation exists. Thus, some parts of the regulation leave room for more specific national rules and in these areas Member States' legislation may vary in respect to both substantive and procedural data protection.

57. Note that the EU Charter of Fundamental Rights (2012/C 326/02, available at: http://eur-lex.europa.eu/legal-content/EN/TXT/?uri=CELEX:12012P/TXT) entrenches to data protection in Art. 8. For the definition of privacy, *see* Ahti Saarenpää: Legal Privacy. In: Ahti Saarenpää (ed.): Legal Privacy. LEFIS Series 5. Prensas Universitarias de Zaragosa. Zaragoza 2008, pp. 19–63.
58. There is sector specific legislation that has an effect on data protection. Note that the Information Society Act (917/2014, in English at: https://www.finlex.fi/fi/laki/kaannokset/2014/en20140917.pdf) that came into force in the beginning of 2015 affects data protection. *See also* the English webpages of the Data Ombudsman, available at: www.tietosuoja.fi/en/index/rekisterinpitajalle.html where the development of legislation for the protection of privacy is explained and relevant acts and decrees listed.
59. Regulation (EU) 2016/679 of the European Parliament and of the Council of Apr. 27, 2016 on the protection of natural persons with regard to the processing of personal data and on the free movement of such data, and repealing Directive 95/46/EC.

Chapter 4. Names

§1. General

65. Names have an important function in the society as they make individuals identifiable from each other. The right to a name is a fundamental right; a part of a person's personality and identity and protected by international conventions (such as the Convention on the Right of a Child, Article 7).

In Finland the naming policy follows the Names Act (694/1985). The act dictates that everyone (a Finnish citizen or a resident) is under an obligation to have a surname (in Finnish: *sukunimi*) and a first name (in Finnish: *etunimi*)(the Names Act, section 1). In other words, names are mandatory in Finland and accordingly, those persons who do not have a name must adopt one when they are entered into the Population Information System. The law gives guidance in respect of deciding, e.g., which names are appropriate and how many names are allowed.[60]

The Ministry of Justice maintains a names committee. It gives opinions for the authorities in name-associated matters.

§2. Surname

I. Acquisition of the Surname

66. The surname can be acquired upon marriage as spouses may decide to share a family name. They are free to choose either woman's or man's surname. However, the surname spouses wish to adopt has to be the surname one of the spouses last had when unmarried (the Names Act, section 8).

It is not mandatory for spouses to choose a common family name. Instead, each spouse may retain the surname that he/she had before the marriage. A third option is to choose—for one of the spouses but not for both of them—a hyphenated, double-barreled surname; this means that a spouse takes his/her own surname in front of the common surname.

67. If spouses want to use a completely new name (usually created by combining parts of their surnames) as their shared family name, permission must be obtained from the Local Registry Office. Permissions have usually been granted if the name is appropriate and not already in use.

68. The surname of a child is inherited and determined by virtue of birth. The Names Act, section 2, provides that if the parents have a common surname at the time of the birth of a child, the child acquires the same surname. The provision is indispositive by nature and therefore no other options for a child's surname is available. If the parents do not have a common surname, the child acquires the surname of either of the parents

60. An English translation can be found at: www.finlex.fi/fi/laki/kaannokset/1985/en19850694.pdf.

that the parents choose. The decision, however, cannot be made freely if the parents have joint custody of another child. In these cases the child acquires at birth the same surname as the sibling has. The notification of the child's surname has to be made to the Population Information System within two months of the child's birth.

If the parents do not share the child's custody, the custodian (custodians) of the child has the right to decide which parent's surname the child gets.

II. Change of the Surname

69. A person residing in Finland and registered in the Finnish Population Register may change his/her family name. Name changes may be made either by submitting an application or notifying a Local Registry Office, depending on the circumstances of each case.

If a spouse has adopted a double-barreled name, it is possible to give it up by notification. One can also adopt a double-barreled name during one's marriage by notifying the Local Registry Office. However, changing spouse's name without an application is available only once during the marriage (the Names Act, section 8a) and one cannot continually switch from a surname to another. This restriction underlines a notion of the important functions that the names have in the Finnish society.

Also a child's name can be changed by notification in cases of, for instance, the establishment of paternity. The requirement is that both of the parents agree that a minor child's surname is changed into the father's surname (*see* the Names Act, sections 4–6).

70. In other cases the main rule is that changing a surname requires submitting an application to the Local Registry Office. Both a need to a change and appropriateness of a new name is considered. According to the Names Act an adequate reason to a change is that the use of the applicant's present surname causes inconvenience due to its foreign origin, its meaning in the standard language or its frequency, or for some other reason (the Names Act, section 10). General impediments to approving a new surname are laid down in the Names Act, section 11. For instance, names that are contrary to the naming practices in Finland cannot be approved.

§3. First Name

71. A person has to have at least one first name. There is also a maximum amount of names as no more than three names may be given to a child after the birth (the Names Act, section 32a). A name may be given at a child's christening or with notification to the Population Information System. Notification must be submitted within two months after the child is born.

Names that are inappropriate or may cause inconvenience cannot be approved. In addition, if a name is a woman's name, it cannot be given to a boy, and vice versa. However, the Names Act is in certain respects quite flexible and allows exceptions to these rules based on, foreign citizenship or religious custom (the Names Act, section 32b).

Chapter 5. Nationality

72. According to the Nationality Act (359/2003),[61] a person may obtain Finnish citizenship (in Finnish: *kansalaisuus*) at birth (a birthplace principle) or through the citizenship of his/her parents (a parentage principle). A child acquires Finnish citizenship at birth for instance in cases where both the child's mother and the father is a Finnish citizen and the parents are married. In an international adoption case, a child under 12 years of age will acquire Finnish citizenship automatically if the adoption is valid in Finland and if at least one of his/her adoptive parents is a Finnish citizen (the Nationality Act, sections 9–11).

73. The Nationality Act includes also provisions by which the social integration of persons residing permanently in Finland is promoted. A citizenship may be acquired by application if the applicant meets certain specific requirements laid down in the section 13 of the Nationality Act. The requirements include—among others—adulthood (reaching the age of 18, or a conclusion of a marriage before this age), meeting the residential period requirement (an applicant must have lived in Finland at least certain period of time) and meeting the integrity requirement (an applicant must not have committed a crime). In addition, an applicant must have sufficient knowledge of either Finnish or Swedish—or Finnish sign language.

A declaration is a simpler way to obtain citizenship than by an application. Persons eligible for citizenship through declaration are defined in the Nationality Act, Chapter 4. For instance, young foreigners who have lived in Finland for a substantial part of their lives and former Finnish citizens, who are Nordic citizens and domiciled in Finland, are eligible for obtaining Finnish citizenship by declaration.[62]

74. Finland has accepted multiple nationality (dual nationality) since 2003. Accordingly a Finnish citizen that acquires a citizenship of another country does not automatically lose a Finnish citizenship. It is possible, thus, to lose a citizenship under certain circumstances and a person may also him/herself request release from the Finnish citizenship.Decisions on obtaining, losing, and retaining the Finnish citizenship are made by the Finnish Immigration Service.[63]

It is noteworthy, thus, that even though obtaining citizenship involves rights and obligations, also the concepts of permanent residence and domicile are of relevance in respect to designating the relation between the individual and the Finnish authorities.

---

61. An English translation of the Nationality Act can be found at: www.finlex.fi/fi/laki/kaannokset/2003/en20030359.pdf. For more information about the Nationality Act and its interpretation, *see* the webpages of the Finnish Immigration Service at: www.migri.fi/finnish_citizenship.
62. For other cases where the method of declaration is possible, *see* the webpages of the Finnish Immigration Service at: www.migri.fi/finnish_citizenship/aged_between_18_and_22.
63. According to Statistics Finland, Finnish citizenship was granted in 2016 to 9,375 foreign citizens permanently resident in Finland. The number is the highest during Finnish independence. Finnish citizenships acquired at birth are not included in these statistics. Official Statistics of Finland: Citizenships, at: www.stat.fi/til/kans/index_en.html.

Chapter 6. Domicile and Habitual Residence

75. Municipalities offer a range of services according to residency in their area. These include for instance health care and day care for children. In order to use the services provided by the municipality, one has to have a residence of a municipality (in Finnish: *kotikunta*) which is determined by the Municipality of Residence Act (201/1994).[64]

Municipality of residence differs from concepts of domicile and habitual residence in private international law. These concepts have not been generally defined in the legislation. In practice it has turned out that defining a person's domicile and/or habitual residence can be very problematic in cross-border cases.

However, there is certain consensus among legal scholars what elements are essential in constituting the concepts in the field of private international law.

76. According to legal literature and case law, both habitual residence and domicile are construed by virtue of the center of a life of a person. This definition refers to a place where a person lives permanently, where he/she works, where he/she have hobbies and social life, where his/her children go to school etc. The concepts of habitual residence and domicile have been traditionally interpreted in a quite similar way compared to each other. Thus, habitual residence changes easier than domicile as it leans purely on facts (past and present) and not the future intentions of the individual. It has been pointed out that in order to acquire a domicile, there should also be willingness and effort to integrate and to settle down to that country. In general, a new habitual residence can be established in a shorter period of time than domicile and without any intentions of staying in a country on a permanent basis.[65]

77. Spouses' domicile and habitual residence are not automatically identical and one does not necessarily follow the other. In addition, the domicile and habitual residence of a child are determined independently from that of his/her parents.

78. It is worth stressing that domicile or habitual residence—as construed in private international law—is not defined by which Population Information System the individual is registered on, but of course registration is taken into account along all other factors when construing the center of one's life.

64. For determining the municipality of residence in cases of immigration or emigration, *see* more closely the webpages of Local Registry Offices at: www.maistraatti.fi/en/Services/place_of_domicile_and_population_data/Basic-information/.

65. Hilkka Salmenkylä: Finland. In: J. Stewart (ed.): Family Law – Jurisdictional Comparisons 2013. Thomson Reuters 2013 pp. 183–200, p. 184.

Part II. Family Law

Chapter 1. Marriage

§1. An Engagement and Its Legal Effects

79. *79.* An engagement (in Finnish: *kihlaus*) is an agreement to marry (the Marriage Act (234/1929), section 1). It can also be defined as a promise of a marriage. The law does not require any special form for an engagement and it is not required to announce it to third parties.

All legal consequences in respect to property relations that an engagement once had according to the Marriage Act (in Finnish: *avioliittolaki*) have been abolished and therefore the rules of property law are normally applied to the parties. Accordingly, if the engagement is broken off, legal consequences may follow the rules of contract and property law. For instance, gifts can exceptionally be claimed back if they were transferred in anticipation of a future commitment and the engagement is terminated by the donee without a proper cause. In the Code of Real Estate (540/1995)[66] there is a special provision concerning the right to revoke the gift (Chapter 4, section 2). Pursuant to it: "If the donee breaches a condition relating to the use of the gift or another essential condition or prerequisite, the donor shall have the right to revoke the gift, unless the donee has conveyed the real estate to a third party. An action for the revocation of gift shall be brought within one year from the donor's gaining knowledge of the grounds for revocation." The provision is applicable to a gift of immovable property.

80. There is no provision in the legislation applicable to revocation of gifts consisting of movable property but according to case law of the Supreme Court (KKO 1991:95), the revocation is possible under exceptional circumstances. If no exceptional circumstances are proven to exist, gifts are binding upon the parties even if given during the engagement that is later broken off.

An engagement may also have legal effects under inheritance law if the other party dies before a conclusion of marriage (before marriage ceremony has taken place). For instance, the Code of Inheritance, Chapter 8, section 2 gives the person who was engaged to the deceased at the time of his/her death, if necessary for his or her livelihood, right to money or other property as a support from the estate. The engagement has

66. In English at: http://www.finlex.fi/fi/laki/kaannokset/1995/en19950540.pdf.

also legal effects according to procedural rules as the fiancé(e) may refuse to give evidence in a court process.

§2. The Capacity to Marry

I. An Examination of Impediments to Marriage

81. An examination of impediments to marriage (in Finnish: *avioliiton esteiden tutkinta*) is an obligatory step that has to be taken before the marriage ceremony. Prospective spouses must together request an examination and it can be presented to the Local Registry Office.[67] The other option is that the impediments are being examined by a parish of the Evangelical-Lutheran Church or the Greek Orthodox Church, but only if those intending to marry or one of them belong to the parish (The Marriage Act, section 10). Prospective spouses have to sign an assurance that to their knowledge there exist no impediments for their marriage (the Marriage Act, section 12).

If no impediments are found, the examiner issues a certificate. Thus, this cannot be done earlier than on the seventh day after the request for an examination of impediments to marriage. The certificate is valid for four months after its issue date and after this the marriage cannot be concluded unless the impediments to marriage have been re-examined (the Marriage Act, section 13).

II. Impediments to Marriage

82. Chapter 2, sections 4–9a of the Marriage Acts states the impediments to marriage. They consist of the following:

- A minor cannot marry and therefore a person must be 18 years of age to conclude a marriage. The Ministry of Justice may, however, for special reasons grant a minor a permission to marry. Before the matter is decided, a custodian has a right to give his/her opinion on the matter, if his or her whereabouts are known or can be determined with reasonable measures. The opinion of the custodian does not bind the authority.
- A person cannot marry if his or her prior marriage or registered partnership is in force.
- A marriage cannot be concluded between close relatives.[68] Therefore, it is not allowed to marry one's direct ascendant or descendant. A marriage is forbidden, i.e., between a child and his/her parent. It is forbidden also between siblings and

67. *See* www.maistraatti.fi/en/Services/marriage/Basic-information/.
68. An adoption creates an impediment to marriage. The adoption Act (22/2012, an English translation can be found at: www.finlex.fi/fi/laki/kaannokset/2012/en20120022.pdf), s. 18 states that once an adoption has been granted, the adoptee shall be deemed the child of the adoptive parents and not of the former parents, unless otherwise expressly provided by law or unless otherwise follows from the nature of adoption.

half-siblings. If one of those intending to marry is a descendant of the other's brother or sister (e.g., uncle and niece), a marriage is thus exceptionally possible under a permission of the Ministry of Justice if special reasons are proved to exist.

83. A legal representative (a guardian) is not competent to give consent to the marriage on behalf of the ward. This underlines the highly personal nature of a marriage (the Guardianship Services Act, section 29). The right for self-determination guarantees that even though a person has a guardian, he/she if free to marry if she/he is able to understand the significance of the institution.

§3. Formalities of Marriage

84. Marriage is a statutory relationship that can be concluded either in a civil marriage ceremony or a religious ceremony. Civil marriages are performed in a Local Registry Office. A church wedding is possible in a religious community that has the right to perform marriage ceremonies (the Marriage Act, section 14). A marriage ceremony is void if performed without the right to perform marriage ceremonies (the Marriage Act, section 19).

Marriage can be concluded only personally and therefore both intending spouses have to be simultaneously present at the ceremony. After both of them have given the officiator of the ceremony an affirmative answer to the question whether he/she wants to marry the other, the officiator pronounces them husband and wife (the Marriage Act, section 15). The legal effects of marriage commence immediately after this.[69]

85. After its conclusion, it is not possible to claim that marriage is not valid according to the contract law. If a spouse regrets the knot he/she has tied, he/she must file for divorce. One must note, though, that if the officiator of the marriage ceremony deems that either of the parties—or both of them—is visibly unable to comprehend the significance of marriage due to some reason (i.e., disturbed state of mind), the officiator may decide not to perform a marriage ceremony. In this respect the officiator has a right to use discretion if one of the intended spouses is for instance under the influence of alcohol or drugs (the Marriage Act, section 18).

According to Statistics Finland's data on population changes, a total of 24,464 marriages were entered into in 2016. The average age of women entering into their first marriage was 31.4 years and 33.7 years for men. The average age of women entering into their second marriage was 44.8 years and 47.6 years for men. Twenty-one percent of all marriages concluded were second marriages, and 4% third marriages.[70]

69. If marriage is concluded with the sole purpose to achieve certain benefits (i.e., residential), and the spouses have agreed i.e., never to live together, the marriage is still valid according to civil law. The prevailing view is that a marriage cannot be declared inefficient because of the "wrong" motives. *See also* a Supreme Court case KKO 2005: 84.
70. Official Statistics of Finland: Changes in marital status, at: www.stat.fi/til/ssaaty/2016/ssaaty_2016_2017-04-20_tie_001_en.html.

§4. Effects of Marriage

I. General

86. The provisions of the Marriage Act have been revised and amended several times over the years. The development has led to the neutrality of spouses' property rights; in other words, the number of provisions that give relevance, in respect to property rights, that the parties are married to each other, has been reduced over the years. Accordingly, at the moment the Marriage Act with regard to property rights of spouses can be defined as a special law, meaning that where the law is silent—and the issue in question is not included in the special notion of matrimonial property regime[71]— the rights of the spouses are evaluated through the glasses of a general system of property rights. Therefore an understanding of property rights between the spouses requires mastering the principles of both matrimonial and property law.[72] In fact, it can be said that during their marriage spouses live in a special contractual relationship.[73]

87. The Marriage Act views and regulates marriage more in economic than emotional terms. Through the amendments a lot of provisions creating obligations by personal nature have been abolished from the Marriage Act. Spouses are equal and independent in respect to their personal matters and therefore free to decide whether he/she wants to go to work, visit family, engage political activities etc.

However, legislation still includes certain rights and duties for spouses that can be defined as personal by nature. The Marriage Act protects the loyalty between the spouses as section 2 states: "The spouses shall be equal. In the marriage, they shall display mutual trust and together work for the good of the family."[74] There are no direct legal consequences if one of the spouses violates obligations arising from this provision and the duties are not enforceable as such.

There are also provisions in the Marriage Act that give protection to the financially weaker spouse. The most important provisions in this respect are those that impose the obligation to maintain the other spouse. The duty to provide maintenance may create financial claims between spouses even during their marriage.

---

71. The notion matrimonial property regime covers the rules concerning marital right and marriage settlements, administration of the property of the spouses, debts of the spouses in inter partes –relation and a distribution of the matrimonial property after death or divorce. Eva Gottberg: Study on Matrimonial Property Regimes and the Property of Unmarried Couples in Private International Law and internal Law. National Report: Finland. Commission Européenne JAI/ A3/2001/03, p. 7.
72. Tuulikki Mikkola: The Risks and Opportunities of Foreign Connections in Marriages: the Proprietary Rights of Spouses. In: B. Atkin (ed.): The International Survey of Family Law, 2008 edition. Jordan Publishing 2008, pp. 77–106, pp. 81–82.
73. Soile Pohjonen: Partnership in Love and Business. Feminist Legal Studies. Vol. 8/2000, pp. 47–63.
74. The s. 2 continues: "Each spouse shall, herself or himself, have the right to decide whether to engage in gainful employment and in societal and other activities outside the family."

II. Property Relations of Spouses

88. Each spouse is equal in relation to personal and financial issues. Both spouses retain financial independence and contractual freedom (in Finnish: *sopimusvapaus*) during marriage (the Marriage Act, section 33), even though each has a marital right to the other spouse's property. Marital right does not, as such, create property rights to the other spouse's property during marriage.[75]

The Marriage Act is based on a freedom of contract and therefore the marriage does not restrict the right of a spouse to administer the property and enter into transactions concerning it.[76] Each spouse has the right to legally bind him/her with third parties and contracts made by the other spouse cannot be hampered by the other spouse's interference. The other spouse has no right to intervene if the other wants to make a transaction with a third party. He or she may, for instance, donate property without the other spouse's approval.[77] The spouses are free to make binding contracts between each other, as well.[78] Also gifts between spouses have a binding effect *inter partes*. Donations between spouses are also valid in respect to third parties.

As spouses retain their property rights and owner's status during marriage, their property is considered separate. The property that a spouse has when marriage is concluded remains his or hers. He or she also owns what he/he acquires during the marriage (the Marriage Act, section 34). Spouses are therefore sole owners of their property; a spouse is considered to own his/her property regardless whether it was acquired before or during the marriage. Marriage does not create a joint estate—or common ownership—between the parties.

---

75. The marital property system is also applied to a registered, same-sex couple. *See* the Act on Registered Partnerships (950/2001, in English at: www.finlex.fi/fi/laki/kaannokset/2001/en20010950.pdf). As the same-sex partners can now get married, it is possible to convert a registered partnership to a marriage. The requirement is that both parties jointly notify their Local Registry Office. Conversion is not obligatory and registered partnerships still continue to exist even though new ones cannot be registered. If a registered partnership is not converted to a marriage, the Act on Registered Partnerships applies.
76. There can be an exception to this rule, if the spouse is going to make a transfer concerning a dwelling that is used as a family, matrimonial home. The marriage restricts the contractual freedom of an owner in these cases and concerning this property (the Marriage Act, ss. 38–39).
77. However, if the property subject to the marital right is administered in a way that it has unnecessarily decreased to the detriment of the other spouse, the decrease may have legal consequences in the distribution of matrimonial property (*see* i.e., the Marriage Act, ss. 37 and 94) as the decrease may lead to a compensation to the other party. It is noteworthy, though, that compensation is not payable during the marriage. In addition, it is not possible to restrict the owner's right to administer his/her property during the marriage even in cases where it is obvious that the transactions will lead to the decrease of the property subject to a marital right.
78. The general requirements concerning the validity or invalidity of contracts apply. A contract may be proved by any means and it is not subject to any requirement as to form. However, for some contracts there are formal requirements. A transfer of immovable property must be in writing, signed and witnessed. Also promises of gifts must be in writing in order to be valid. A party is not bound by a contract that the other party has obtained by fraud, duress or undue influence. *See* more closely O. Lando et al. (eds.): Restatement of Nordic Contract Law. Djof Publishing 2016, pp. 26–27.

89. The general rules of ownership apply also between spouses, unless otherwise specifically provided by the Marriage Act. Therefore the starting point is that a spouse's ownership to a certain property is determined according to the general principles of property law. If spouses have acquired property jointly, co-ownership (in Finnish: *yhteisomistus*) is created and the Act on Common Ownership (180/1958) is applicable. According to it, co-owners shares to the object are specified and fractional. Shares are equal between co-owners unless agreed otherwise between the co-owners at the time of the conveyance of the object. Co-owner has a right to assign his or her share and dispose of it freely.[79] The act applies also to spouses unless otherwise stated in the Marriage Act. Thus, in sections 65 and 89 of the Marriage Act there are provisions concerning *presumption* of ownership of movable property between spouses—but these are applicable only in cases where there are no specific agreements stating otherwise.

90. Each spouse is free to administer his/her property and if the spouses own property jointly, they naturally also have to administer such property together. The marriage does not create a right to make legal transactions that concern the other spouse's property without permission from the owner. There is a provision in the Marriage Act stating explicitly (section 58) that if a spouse alienates or pledges movable property belonging to the other spouse (or property i.e., owned jointly by the spouses) without the consent of the other spouse, the latter has the right to redeem it. If the third party was not in good faith, or if the legal transaction was not for consideration, the spouse is entitled to regain the property without redemption.

Also liability for debts remain separate and a spouse cannot be held liable for a debt of the other spouse whether incurred before or during the marriage. Thus, for debts incurred for the maintenance of the family, spouses are jointly liable. This is the only exception to the main rule and it is not ever applied to a monetary loan taken out by a spouse nor if the creditor knew that the spouses were separated due to a breakdown of their relationship (the Marriage Act, section 52). Naturally, if spouses have incurred a debt together during the marriage, they are jointly and severally liable for it. The rule is corresponding to the general regulation on joint debts.[80]

III. Maintenance

91. During the marriage, both spouses are obliged to participate in the common household of the family and the maintenance (in Finnish: *elatus*) of the spouses to the

79. According to the Act on Common Ownership (180/1958) the dissolution of the co-ownership is possible upon the request of a co-owner (s. 9.2). The court may order the object to be sold and its price to be divided among the co-owners (proportionate to their shares, naturally). This procedure is open to spouses as well, as long as their marriage lasts, if there are no grounds to start a distribution of matrimonial property.

80. Eva Gottberg: Study on Matrimonial Property Regimes and the Property of Unmarried Couples in Private International Law and internal Law. National Report: Finland. Commission Européenne JAI/A3/2001/03, p. 8.

best of his/her abilities (the Marriage Act, section 46).[81] The maintenance of the spouses includes fulfillment of the common needs of the spouses as well as the personal, essential needs of each spouse. Maintenance covers all reasonable costs of living, such as food, housing, clothing, medical treatment, etc.

The extent of the maintenance is not in detail regulated by the law. However, the "best of his or her abilities" refers to a possibility that there are different ways to support the family and the ways of fulfilling the obligation may vary between the spouses—depending whether or not a spouse engages gainful employment outside of a home. If so, then usually the spouse supports the other by giving him or her part of the salary in case the other spouse stays at home.

92. Housework is also considered one way to participate in the common household and the maintenance of the spouses. Accordingly, a spouse is not supposed to be compensated for the homework as he/she is rather fulfilling the maintenance obligation. However, if a spouse is employed in the other spouse's firm, salary has to be paid if it was intended or agreed upon—or that its payment, with a view to the nature of the work and the other circumstances, is deemed reasonable (the Marriage Act, section 64).[82] The Marriage Act also provides that if no compensation was agreed upon, it is possible to bring an action therefore. One should react quite fast as this should be done within a year from the end of the calendar year during which the work was performed. Compensation paid after this is deemed a gift.

93. If the obligation to support is not fulfilled, it is possible—even during the marriage—to raise a claim for the confirmation of the amount of the maintenance in a court (the Marriage Act, section 49). The amount of the maintenance and method of payment can also be confirmed by an agreement between the spouses. A court may order a maintenance to be payable retroactively but only for a period not exceeding the year prior to the bringing of the action (the Marriage Act, section 49).

As mentioned earlier, there is one irregularity concerning separate liability of debts between spouses. According to the Marriage Act, section 52, both spouses are jointly and severally liable for a debt incurred by a spouse for the maintenance of the family.[83] There are, thus, exceptions to this rule as a spouse is not liable for a debt for the maintenance of the family if the spouses have separated due to a breakdown of their relationship and if the creditor was aware of the separation. Furthermore, monetary loans are never regarded as maintenance loans in applying this provision; according to the judicial practice, the same applies to credit card loans even though it can be proved that the credit was used for household expenses.

---

81. The maintenance regulation concerning a right of a child to receive maintenance from his or her parents is considered as a separate issue from the obligation to support one's spouse. Regulation concerning maintenance of children is included in the Act on Child Maintenance (704/1975).
82. Kirsti Kurki-Suonio: Property Relationship Between Spouses—Finland. Commission on European Family Law: Country Reports 2008, p. 6.
83. Kirsti Kurki-Suonio: Property Relationship Between Spouses—Finland. Commission on European Family Law: Country Reports, 2008, p. 6, gives an example of a maintenance debt and writes: "...a dentist's bill concerning one spouse's dental care can be considered to the a debt for the maintenance of the family, of which both of the spouses are jointly and severally liable according to § 52(2) of Finnish Marriage Act."

94. There is an interesting Supreme Court decision KKO 2008:66 concerning the definition and extent of maintenance. Spouses had, during their marriage, rented a flat together to be used as their common, family home. Later, when they separated and the other spouse moved away due to the breakdown of their relationship, the other spouse paid the whole rent for about a half year's time. The spouse who had paid the rent claimed that the other spouse was liable for paying back half of it. The Supreme Court found that the liability to pay the rent of a spouses' matrimonial home had to be considered as against a liability to support and provide maintenance according to the Marriage Act, sections 46–51. The claim of the spouse was rejected because it was based on general civil law; instead, it should have been based on the maintenance obligation arising out of the marriage.

IV. Last Name of the Spouses

95. Those intending to marry may choose to keep their own last names (the Names Act, section 8). It is also possible to adopt a common last name but only if the surname is one that either of the spouses last had when unmarried. A name which one of the spouses gained in his/her previous marriage cannot be chosen as a common name. The spouse whose name is about to change may also use his/her former last name before the common last name (so-called double-barreled surname, the Names Act, section 7). This may only be a personal choice as the option is not open for both of the spouses and accordingly, a double-barreled surname can only be adopted by one of the spouses.[84]

The officiator of the ceremony has to be notified of the choice of a common last name before the ceremony (the Names Act, section 7).

§5. Void and Voidable Marriages

96. The Marriage Act does not include provisions on void and voidable marriages (such as nullification) as divorce and death of a spouse are only ways how a marriage is dissolved.[85] Even if one of the spouses is mentally ill and unable to understand the legal effects of the marriage ceremony, it is not possible to cancel the marriage afterward.

In addition, even if a marriage has been concluded despite the existence of mandatory impediment to the marriage, there are no provisions in the law on the *ex nunc* annulment of a marriage. Also these marriages are therefore dissolved by divorce

84. If a spouse has chosen a double-barreled surname, he/she can relinquish the first surname during a marriage or, a spouse may also adopt a double-barreled surname during a marriage, by making a written announcement to the Local Registry Office (the Names Act, s. 8a).

85. In a Supreme Administrative Court case KHO 2003:69 the marriage was concluded in the Local Registry Office. A spouse applied an annulment of the marriage (decision) based on the Administrative Judicial Procedure Act (586/1996), s. 63. The court reasoned that an officiator of a civil marriage ceremony does not make an administrative decision covered by the act and therefore the annulment was not an alternate way to end the marriage.

but without a reconsideration period. A public prosecutor may initiate proceedings for the divorce of the spouses in such cases (the Marriage Act, section 27).[86]

86. The Marriage Act, s. 27 can be applied in cases where the spouses are each other's direct descendants or ascendants, siblings or half-siblings, or if their marriage was concluded while a prior marriage or registered partnership of one of the spouses was still in force, and the said prior marriage or registered partnership has not yet been dissolved. *See* Matti Savolainen: Grounds for Divorce and Maintenance Between Former Spouses (Finland). Commission on European Family Law: Country Reports, 2002, pp. 3–4.

Chapter 2. Divorce

§1. Grounds

97. The divorce system in force was adopted in 1987. The amendment of the system led to bringing the principle of divorce on demand to the Marriage Act. Such concepts as a fault and disreputable conduct were eliminated from it.[87] The system respects the privacy of the parties as spouses' personal relationship and nature of their marriage is not relevant when the court is handling divorce (in Finnish: *avioero*). Divorce—as it is regulated nowadays—has been acclaimed as being humane, smooth-running and inexpensive.[88]

A divorce becomes pending in the District Court by a written application. It can be made by either both of the spouses or by one spouse alone. In the latter case the consent of the other spouse is not required. Accordingly, it is not possible that a spouse prevents the other spouse from obtaining a divorce by objecting to it (the Marriage Act, sections 25–26).

In case the spouses—or one of them—decide to end their marriage, after a reconsideration period (in Finnish: *harkinta-aika*) of at least six months, the application must be renewed by both spouses or just one of them. Again, there is no need to prove any grounds—or investigate the circumstances—at this stage of the procedure. The original applicant cannot withdraw the application he/she has submitted to the court. Thus, the divorce case lapses if the second request is not submitted to a court within one year of the beginning of the reconsideration period. In this case the marriage continues normally.

98. As a rule, a reconsideration period is required. However, there are few exceptions to this rule. If the spouses have de facto lived apart for a period of at least two years without interruptions, each spouse is entitled to apply for an immediate divorce without the period of reconsideration (the Marriage Act, section 25). Again, in these cases the reasons for the separation do not have to be stipulated. It is irrelevant whether the spouses are still attached to each other or the separation has been caused

87. For a brief history of the divorce law *see* for instance Matti Savolainen: Grounds for Divorce and Maintenance Between Former Spouses (Finland). Commission on European Family Law: Country Reports, 2002, p. 2. For developments toward a more streamlined forms of divorce in Nordic countries, *see* Mary-Ann Glendon: The Transformation of Family Law: State, Law, and Family in the United States and Western Europe. University of Chicago Press 1989, pp. 185–188.

88. Matti Savolainen: Grounds for Divorce and Maintenance Between Former Spouses (Finland). Commission on European Family Law: Country Reports, 2002, p. 3. He provides the reader with an opinion that "a more restrictive divorce system seems to be politically out of the question."

by a breakdown of their personal relations. In addition, an immediate divorce is available if a marriage was concluded while a former marriage was still in force.[89]

It is noteworthy that to obtain the divorce, it is not necessary that the marriage has lasted for a certain time. A divorce can even be applied as soon as the marriage ceremony is over.

According to Statistics Finland's data on population changes in 2016, first marriages end in divorce with a probability of 39%. The median for the duration of first marriages ending in divorce was ten years. Seven out of ten of the marriages that ended in divorce in 2016 were first marriages for both spouses.[90]

§2. Mediation

99. Mediation is not a mandatory phase in connection with divorce proceedings. However, the Marriage Act contains provisions on special out of court family mediation service. Accordingly the idea is that disputes (including legal consequences following divorce) arising within a family should primarily be settled in voluntary negotiations between the members of the family and decided by agreement (the Marriage Act, section 20).

In all cases contacting and commencing mediation service is voluntary. Mediation is cost-free and is arranged by the municipal social welfare officers. Also those associations and individuals who are authorized to provide the services are entitled to arrange family mediation (the Marriage Act, sections 22–23).[91]

100. Mediation services are flexibly available at any stage of the divorce proceedings, before the divorce application has been submitted or after, during the divorce proceedings and even after the divorce has been granted. A mediator strives for a consensus that is acceptable from the perspectives of all the persons concerned. However, the mediator has to pay special attention how to secure the position of the minor children in the family in a best possible way (the Marriage Act, section 21).

Where mediation is successful, all de facto consequences of divorce, such as maintenance for the children, their custody and visiting rights and the division of matrimonial property may be settled and decided by an enforceable out of court

89. According to the Marriage Act, s. 27, the public prosecutor is able to initiate proceedings for the divorce of the spouses upon certain grounds; namely, if the spouses are each other's direct descendants or ascendants, siblings or half-siblings; or if their marriage was concluded while a prior marriage or registered partnership of one of the spouses was still in force, and the said prior marriage or registered partnership has not yet been dissolved. In these cases the divorce is granted without a reconsideration period.

90. Official Statistics of Finland: Changes in marital status, at: www.stat.fi/til/ssaaty/2016/ssaaty_2016_2017-04-20_tie_001_en.html.

91. Spouses may have conversations either alone or together with i.e., a social worker. In family mediation, the negotiations are confidential. Hilkka Salmenkylä: Finland. In: J. Stewart (ed.): Family Law – Jurisdictional Comparisons 2013. Thomson Reuters 2013 pp. 183–200, p. 198. *See also* the webpages of Judicial Administration at: oikeus.fi/en/index/esitteet/avioliittolaki/perheasioidensovittelu.html.

agreement between the spouses.[92] The alternative is that the spouses leave these matters unresolved and initiate separate judicial proceedings at a later stage.[93]

In practice, mediation services are not usually found and they are quite seldom utilized by the spouses facing problems in their marriage—even in cases where they end up in requesting divorce.

§3. Procedure

I. General

101. Divorce proceedings are initiated in the court of the first instance, by a written and signed application. It is possible that a spouse requests divorce alone or that both spouses request divorce together.[94] In the former case, the court serves the petition on the other spouse and reserves him or her an opportunity to issue a statement on it. However, it is not possible to successfully object the petition for instance on subjective grounds. Legally it is irrelevant whether there exist valid reasons obtaining a divorce or not. In addition, the application does not require that spouses have agreed on financial and other consequences following divorce. Spouses have an independent and absolute right to file for a divorce (the Marriage Act, section 25).

The reconsideration period begins upon the date when the joint petition of the spouses for the dissolution of the marriage is filed with the court or the court registry or the petition of one spouse is served on the other spouse (the Marriage Act, section 26). After six-months-time has lapsed, either of the spouses may request a divorce in a court by a written and signed application. If either of the spouses—or both—renews the application after the six months' period, the divorce is granted. If the spouses want a final divorce, the petition has to be filed within one year of the beginning of the reconsideration period (the Marriage Act, section 26). A decree of divorce granted by the district court becomes final after the expiry of a seven-day period after the decree was granted and no appeal has been lodged.[95]

102. If the petition is based on the de facto separation for at least two years, the divorce may be granted immediately, without the reconsideration period. Again, it is irrelevant what are and has been the reasons for the separation. According to the judicial practice the burden of proof is not set high in respect to proving the actual separation of the spouses. Therefore, in most cases presenting an extract from the Population Information System is enough and witnesses do not have to appear before the court

---

92. Matti Savolainen: Grounds for Divorce and Maintenance Between Former Spouses (Finland). Commission on European Family Law: Country Reports, 2002, p. 8.
93. Hilkka Salmenkylä: Finland. In: J. Stewart (ed.): Family Law – Jurisdictional Comparisons 2013. Thomson Reuters 2013 pp. 183–200, p. 187.
94. The petition may be taken to the registry of the district court personally or sent to the court by mail, fax or e-mail. *See* the webpages of Judicial Administration at: oikeus.fi/tuomioistuimet/karajaoikeudet/en/index/hakemusasiat/perheasiat/divorce.html.
95. Matti Savolainen: Grounds for Divorce and Maintenance Between Former Spouses (Finland). Commission on European Family Law: Country Reports, 2002, p. 6.

to testify that the required separation has taken place. Usually the court is satisfied if the spouses together assure that they have been living apart, unless there seem to exist reasons according to which the truthfulness of the statements may be doubted.[96]

In addition, a divorce is granted without a reconsideration period if the marriage has been concluded even though there existed an impediment for a marriage. According to the Marriage Act, section 27 the public prosecutor has to initiate proceedings for the divorce if the marriage was concluded between close relatives—or if the marriage was concluded while a prior marriage (or a registered partnership) of one of the spouses was still in force, and the said prior marriage or registered partnership has not yet been dissolved.

II. Other Matters to Be Dealt with in Connection with a Divorce

103. In connection with a divorce, it is possible to claim certain other matters to be dealt with in a court, in case these are related to a divorce case of the parties. Such are for instance custody of a child and maintenance payable to a child or a spouse.[97] A spouse may also claim an appointment of an estate distributor to carry out the distribution of matrimonial property. These matters may also be claimed and decided in a court in separate proceedings and not in connection with a divorce.

A spouse may also submit an application for a court order on the end of cohabitation (the Marriage Act, section 24). By such an order it is determined which of the spouses needs a residence more and who therefore is entitled to continue living in the common home. The order gives a spouse the right to use the household goods and also movables meant for his/her personal use. The other spouse has to vacate the common home. In this respect it is irrelevant who is the owner of the property in question.

104. The rights that are based on the order on the end of cohabitation cannot be restricted by an agreement that is entered into by the owner of the said property and a third party.

The order is in force until the distribution of matrimonial property (upon divorce) has been carried out.[98] There is also a general timeframe as in any case the order lapses in two years. It is noteworthy, though, that the order does not require divorce proceedings and it can be applied for and given even during the marriage. The order—or claiming it—does not initiate divorce proceedings, either.

96. For the required evidence of the de facto separation *see* Matti Savolainen: Grounds for Divorce and Maintenance Between Former Spouses (Finland). Commission on European Family Law: Country Reports, 2002, pp. 3–4. Savolainen has noted that as a consequence of a low burden of proof, even these cases are usually decided upon in chambers.

97. The parents may also agree the matters concerning their children by concluding an agreement. If the social welfare authority confirms the agreement, it binds as a court decision. Without such confirmation, an agreement on children is not enforceable.

98. A spouse may also request for a change or revocation of an order in a court, if the circumstances have changed after the order was issued.

§4. EFFECTS

I. Maintenance

105. The duty to maintain one's spouse lasts until the final divorce decree is issued; in most cases after the reconsideration period. The supportive bond between spouses breaks in divorce and afterward both parties have to make one's own living. This was confirmed in the precedent of the Supreme Court KKO 2004:104. According to the decision, the divorced spouse is liable to pay maintenance to his/her ex-spouse only rarely and only if the claimant is not able to support him/herself and the inability occurs because of the marriage. Naturally, it is also required that the other spouse is capable of paying the maintenance and that the duty to pay support is reasonable in light of the circumstances of the case. The marital bond itself is not a reason to pay maintenance to the other spouse after the marital bond ceases to exist.[99]

Nonetheless, in a Supreme Court case KKO 2010:3, a claim for maintenance after the divorce was accepted. The circumstances of the case were exceptional as the claimant was the wife who was of foreign origin and did not speak fluent Finnish. In addition, she did not have any professional training. The marriage had lasted for ten years. Family home had been in Finland during all this time. Wife had given birth to three children and taken care of their upbringing. In divorce children stayed with their father. The Supreme Court stated that in this case it was proven that the wife was not able to support herself and the inability occurred because of the marriage. The husband was ordered to pay (a relatively small sum of) maintenance each month for three years' time, starting from the divorce.[100]

106. Again, spouses may during their marriage, within their contractual freedom, enter into an agreement according to which maintenance is payable upon divorce. If the social welfare authority has confirmed the contract, it is enforceable. Thus, an agreement on support and maintenance between the spouses can be amended if it is considered to be unreasonable. If the matter cannot be agreed by the parties, it can be brought to the district court.

In all cases duty to pay maintenance ceases if the person entitled to maintenance after divorce remarries (the Marriage Act, section 48).

---

99. A court may order maintenance to be paid retroactively for a period not exceeding the year prior to the bringing of the action, *see* the Marriage Act, s. 49.

100. It is at the court's discretion to determine the amount of maintenance. The court also has to use discretion to make a decision on how maintenance is payable and for how long. If the financial circumstances of the liable party justify it, the maintenance can be ordered payable even in a lump sum. If a court has ordered maintenance to be payable in a lump sum, the order (or agreement specifying a lump sum maintenance payment) cannot be changed after the maintenance has been paid. For details of calculating maintenance *see* Matti Savolainen: Grounds for Divorce and Maintenance Between Former Spouses (Finland). Commission on European Family Law: Country Reports, 2002, pp. 12–17.

II. Distribution of Matrimonial Property

107. When a marriage is dissolved either by a divorce or a death of a spouse, the principle of separate ownership is not applied as such since each spouse have a marital right (in Finnish: *avio-oikeus*) to the property of the other spouse (the Marriage Act, section 35). The marital right gives each spouse certain rights to property of the other spouse when the matrimonial property is distributed.

The marital right is a special property right that is enforced only when the matrimonial property is distributed. It has no legal effects or any economical value as long the marriage persists. Therefore, a marital right cannot, for instance, be donated or sold to a third party.

Chapter 3. Cohabitation Without Marriage

§1. General

108. During the 1970s cohabitation (in Finnish: *avoliitto*) became a quite popular alternative to marriage as a form of a relationship. At first it was considered to precede marriage. Over the years, however, cohabitation has turned to an institution that may be a permanent way of living and not just a first step toward knotting the marital bond.[101]

The Act on the Dissolution of the Household of Cohabiting Partners (26/2011) is applicable when partnership ends (the Act on the Dissolution of the Household of Cohabiting Partners, section 1). The act applies both to opposite and same-sex partnerships. The provisions of the act do not create any personal or economical rights and/or duties that would have legal effect as long as the partnership persists.

109. The rights and duties of cohabiting partners are not comparable to the rights of married spouses and therefore, provisions of the Marriage Act are not applicable to cohabitation even by way of analogy. Cohabitees are not, for example, obliged to maintain each other. The cohabitation does not create a marital right to the property owned by the other cohabitee. Accordingly, the purpose of the Act on the Dissolution of the Household of Cohabiting Partners is to protect the rights of cohabiting partners only at the time when the partnership ends. The owner may therefore administer and dispose of his/her property as he/she wishes—even when property that is being disposed of is used as a common home of the family.[102]

As a rule, the act on the Dissolution of the Household of Cohabiting Partners is not applicable if the cohabitation has lasted for a short time. It is provided in the act that it applies only if the partners have lived in a shared household for at least five years. Exceptionally the act is applicable also if the cohabitation has lasted for a shorter period of time if the partners have, or have had, a joint child or joint parental responsibility for a child.[103] The act does not apply if both of the partners (or one of them) are married (the Act on the Dissolution of the Household of Cohabiting Partners, section 3).

110. The provisions of the Act on the Dissolution of the Household of Cohabiting Partners are usually non-mandatory and parties may derogate from them by a mutual

101. For the development of quasi-marital relationships, *see* Klaus Törnudd: Finland and the International Norms of Human Rights. Martinus Nijhoff Publishers 1986, p. 107. For the number of cohabiting couples with and without children, *see* Official Statistics of Finland: Families, at: www.stat.fi/til/perh/2016/perh_2016_2017-05-26_tie_001_en.html.

102. *See* Salla Silvola: National Report: Informal Relationships – Finland. Commission on European Family Law: Country Reports, 2015, p. 19.

103. Sometimes it is not easy to define when the continuous cohabitation can be deemed to begin. Interpretation of the factual circumstances is therefore crucial. In practice, one usually relies on the fact when cohabitees submitted a notification of the change of address in the population register. Also, it can be very problematic to define a moment when a cohabitation ends/has ended. *See* Salla Silvola: National Report: Informal Relationships – Finland. Commission on European Family Law: Country Reports, 2015, pp. 5–6.

agreement. Their contractual freedom is, however, limited in some respects. The cohabiting partner—or the heir of a deceased cohabiting partner—may not validly waive his/her right to demand the separation of property or his or her right to apply for an appointment of an estate distributor (the Act on the Dissolution of the Household of Cohabiting Partners, section 2).

§2. Separation of the Property upon Dissolution of the Common Household

111. Under the Act on the Dissolution of the Household of Cohabiting Partners, it is possible to demand the separation of property in case the partnership ends. Separation of property can be made by an agreement but if the parties are unable to find an agreeable end-result, it is possible for each of them to apply for an estate distributor (in Finnish: *pesänjakaja*) in a district court. The distributor carries out the separation of the property. It is noteworthy, though, that the main responsibility and task of an estate distributor is to strive an end-result where the parties would agree on the separation of property.

In separation both partners keep what they own. The distributor cannot make changes to property ownership. Either is the estate distributor able to transfer property ownership between the partners. Therefore, property is usually divided in accordance with what belongs to whom. In this respect general rules of property law apply.[104] In cases where it is not possible to establish who owns a specific, movable item, partners are presumed to own it together as the Act on the Dissolution of the Household of Cohabiting Partners, section 6, states: "If, when separating the property, the agreement between the cohabiting partners or the circumstances otherwise do not indicate and it cannot be proved which cohabiting partner a moveable object belongs to or that it is joint property, the partners are deemed as having acquired it jointly with equal rights." It must be noted, though, that this provision applies only if the property is being separated in the context of the dissolution of the common household. The provision is not intended to solve contested ownerships of partners who are still living together with no intention of dissolving their relationship. For them, the general rules of property law apply.

§3. Compensation

112. A cohabiting partner can be entitled to compensation (in Finnish: *hyvitys*). The requirements for compensation are laid down in the Act on the Dissolution of the Household of Cohabiting Partners, section 8. A right to compensation exists if either of the partners—through a contribution for the benefit of the common household—has assisted the other partner in retaining or accumulating his or her property. In addition,

---

104. A question of ownership is important in a termination of relationship. In addition to the title, the Supreme Court has paid attention to the common intention of the partners. For example, in a Supreme Court decision KKO 2016:37 it was held to be decisive what the parties had agreed on the ownership at the moment of conveyance.

it has to be shown that the separation of property solely on the basis of ownership would result in enrichment at the expense of the other.

The above-mentioned provision includes also a list of what can be deemed to be the contributions for the benefit of a shared household when considering whether there exists a right to compensation. The list includes work done by one cohabiting partner for the benefit of the shared household or property owned by the other. Furthermore, the use of funds for the shared household and investment of funds by one cohabiting partner in property owned by the other can considered to be such contributions that may lead to compensation. No right to compensation exists, however, if the unjust enrichment is considered as insignificant.

113. The compensation belongs to the sphere of contractual freedom of the parties and they may always agree on it. In case they cannot reach a shared understanding on the matter, an estate distributor makes decisions on compensation that has been claimed.[105] If an application to appoint an estate distributor has not been made, a claim for compensation can also be submitted directly to the district court. The compensation can be claimed within six months of the separation of the property. In case the parties have decided that there is no need for a separation procedure, the right to claim compensation lapses in three years of the date the partners have moved permanently apart or of the death of the partner (the Act on the Dissolution of the Household of Cohabiting Partners, section 9).[106]

114. As a rule, a cohabitating partner does not have a right to inherit unless there is a will for his/her benefit. However, a partner is able to receive discretionary support from the estate of the deceased partner according to the Inheritance Code, Chapter 8, section 2, but only if it is deemed reasonable under the circumstances. The support may also be paid in the form of a right to use the property.

105. If the other party claims that there is an agreement concerning the compensation and an estate distributor has been appointed, it is his/her duty to examine the validity of it. If it is considered valid, it binds the distributor. Under exceptional circumstances the agreement may be adjusted due to its unfairness, according to the Contracts Act s. 36. Salla Silvola: National report: Informal Relationships – Finland. Commission on European Family Law: Country Reports, 2015, p. 31.

106. In case the Act on the Dissolution of the Household of Cohabiting Partners is not applicable, there is no statutory equalization of property upon termination of a relationship. Instead general provisions of civil law apply. If either of the cohabiting partners has made financial or other contributions to the other partner's property, he/she may raise a claim based on unjust enrichment. A claim is raised on the district court as the appointment is of an estate distributor is not possible if the Act on the Dissolution of the Household of Cohabiting Partners is not applicable.

Chapter 4. Filiation

§1. General

115. Motherhood and fatherhood are both basic institutions in a welfare society. The establishment of a biological bond between a child and a parent has important legal consequences. Child law encompasses such issues—among others—as maintenance, custody and the right of access.

A right to know one's biological origin is also a part of one's personal identity and is protected as a basic right. This follows from, for instance, the United Nations Convention on the Rights of the Child as its Article 7 states: "The child shall be registered immediately after birth and shall have the right from birth to a name, the right to acquire a nationality and, as far as possible, the right to know and be cared for by his or her parents." In Finland paternity is a legal construction whereas motherhood is still considered legally as a fact. Law provides no regulation concerning a child's origin on the mother's side.

In child law a basic approach to the legal status of a child is that he/she is an independent legal subject, also in relation to his/her parents. Yet, from the perspective of paternity, it is still relevant whether a child's mother is married when giving birth. Cohabitation as such does not create presumption of paternity. Each year, however, more than 40% of children are born to parents who are not married. In 2015, the paternity of 23,580 children born out of wedlock was established.[107] It is also noteworthy that there are some 106,000 people in Finland who have no legally registered father.[108]

§2. Children Born in Wedlock

116. According to the Paternity Act (11/2015)[109] the husband is the father of a child, when a child is born in marriage. It is irrelevant for how long the marriage had lasted before the child was born and whether it had been biologically possible that a child was conceived during the marriage.

If the husband dies before the birth of the child, the deceased is considered to be the father of the child if the child was born within a time that the child could have been conceived before the death of the husband. However, if the mother had concluded

107. According to statistics collected by National institute for Health and Welfare, the possibility of establishing paternity through acknowledgement is used in most cases. *See* Statistical report 11/2016, 26 May 2016 Official Statistics of Finland, Child Maintenance and Custody. THL, at: www.thl.fi/en/web/thlfi-en/statistics/statistics-by-topic/social-services-children-adolescents-and-families/child-maintenance-and-custody. For statistics concerning different types of families, *see* Official Statistics of Finland: Families, at: www.stat.fi/til/perh/2016/perh_2016_2017-05-26_tie_001_en.html.

108. Yle News, at: yle.fi/uutiset/osasto/news/new_rights_upcoming_for_biological_fathers/5303430.

109. Published in English at: www.finlex.fi/fi/laki/kaannokset/2015/en20150011.pdf.

a new marriage before the birth of the child, the current husband is the father of the child (the Paternity Act, section 2). Again, it is irrelevant for how long the marriage had lasted before the birth of a child. In this respect the law sees the paternity more as a legal (in addition to social) construction than a biological fact.

As a rule, therefore, the husband remains as the child's father. It is possible, though, that a man, other than a husband, is confirmed as the father. Yet, this requires that both spouses have accepted it. A man (in this case a plaintiff), other than the husband, could also request the annulment of the husband's paternity. Under the Paternity Act, section 42, the requirements are that the mother and the husband did not live together at the time the child was born whereas the plaintiff had lived together with the mother of the child at the time the child was born and participated in the care of the child. Accordingly, it has to be proven that a family bond has been formed between the plaintiff and the child. The court also has to evaluate what is the result that is in the best interests of the child.

§3. Children Born Out of Wedlock

117. If the paternity is not determined on the basis of a marriage, it is established by a decision of the Local Registry Office or the district court. A man can acknowledge his paternity already during the pregnancy at a maternity clinic. After the birth there exists certain time limit (thirty days) during which the man can cancel the acknowledgment of his paternity (the Paternity Act, section 16).

118. Following the child's birth, paternity can be acknowledged at a child supervisor's office. The child supervisor investigates paternity when he/she has been informed of an under-aged child whose paternity has not been determined on the basis of marriage and a man wants to acknowledge paternity. There are provisions covering the investigation of paternity in the Paternity Act, Chapter 2. The investigation refers to procedures in order to obtain enough information on the basis of which paternity can be established or determined. Usually, the investigation is conducted after the birth of a child (the Paternity Act, section 4).[110] The acknowledgment of paternity is confirmed at the Local Registry Office (*see* the Paternity Act, Chapter 5).

If the assumed father of the child does not voluntarily acknowledge his paternity, it is possible to bring an action against him for the confirmation of paternity. If the man has deceased, the action is brought against the legal successors of the man (the Paternity Act, section 29).

110. Investigation of paternity is possible also in cases, where the mother of the child and the man whose paternity has been determined on the basis of marriage agree to the investigation of paternity since another man has acknowledged paternity or informs that he will do so. *See* the Paternity Act, s. 4.

Chapter 5. Adoption

119. The Adoption Act (22/2012) includes provisions on how to transfer a parentage by an adoption. The purpose of the act is to promote the welfare of minor children in adoption issues (the Adoption Act, section 1). The Adoption Act, section 2 reads, "in all decisions and other measures concerning the adoption of a minor child, the best interests of the child shall be the paramount consideration." Under the act, it is also possible to adopt an adult (*see* the Adoption Act, section 4).

The Adoption Act lays down provisions on conditions for adoption. A minor child may be adopted if it is considered to be in the best interests of the child. Furthermore, it has to be proven that the child will be well taken care of and brought up. The child has to be heard and his/her wishes and views have to be taken into consideration in the process (having regard to his or her age and degree of maturity, the Adoption Act, section 3). If a child has reached 12 years of age, an adoption may not be granted without the child's consent. It is further stated in the Adoption Act that also in cases where an adoptee is younger than 12 years of age, an adoption may not be granted against his/her will if the child is deemed to be mature enough that his or her will can be taken into consideration (the Adoption Act, section 10).

120. The minimum age of the prospective adopter is 25 years, and it may not exceed 50 years. In addition, if the adoptee is a minor, the age difference between the adoptee and the adopter must be at least 18 years but cannot exceed 45 years. The rules concerning the age and the age difference may be derogated from under certain exceptional circumstances, such as in cases where the adoptee is the child of the adopter's spouse or the adopter's own child who has previously been adopted by someone else (*see* the Adoption Act, sections 6–7).

Only married spouses—not for instance cohabiting partners—may adopt jointly. Moreover, spouses may not adopt a child in any other way than jointly. There are, however, exceptions to this rule, as stated in the Adoption Act, section 8. A spouse may, for instance, alone adopt a child of the other spouse.

121. An adoption requires the prior consent of the adoptees' parents (the Adoption Act, section 11).[111] There are exceptions to this rule, though. An adoption may be granted without the either of the parent's consent if it can be considered that the adoption strongly serves the best interests of the child. In addition, it is required that there are no sufficient grounds for the denial or withdrawal of consent, when the degree of contact between the child and the parent and the nature of their relationship is taken into account.

The adoption of a minor child requires adoption counseling and following it, permission from the Adoption Board. As a rule, once an adoption has been granted, the adoptee is deemed the child of the adoptive parents and not a child of the former (birth) parents who are for instance discharged from their obligation to maintain the child (the Adoption Act, sections 18–19). An adoption cannot be revoked but its effects may be terminated by a new adoption.

111. Note that there is a mandatory period of reflection according to s. 15 of the Act. Accordingly, a parent's consent to an adoption may not be received until the parent has had the opportunity to consider the matter thoroughly and eight weeks have elapsed from the birth of the child.

It is also possible to adopt a foreign child. The expert body in intercountry adoption matters is the Finnish Board of Inter-Country Adoption Affairs (the Adoption Board). The Adoption Board is the central authority as referred to in The Hague Convention on Protection of Children and Co-operation in Respect of Intercountry Adoption (Treaty SopS 29/1997) and the competent national authority as referred to in the European Convention on the Adoption of Children (Treaty SopS 39/2012).[112]

112. The Adoption Board works under Valvira, the National Supervisory Authority of Welfare and Health. For more information concerning the intercountry adoptions and the work of the Adoption Board *see* Finnish Adoption Board Annual Report 2016, at: www.valvira.fi/documents/18508/3375901/Finnish_Adoption_Board_Annual_Report_2016.pdf/4a3cdca4-50f4-4e1b-6130-624135663bb0. The report shows that the number of intercountry adoption applicants has gradually declined year after year and in 2016, only approximately sixty children came to Finland via intercountry adoption service providers. The number was 308 in 2005.

Chapter 6. Parental Authority

§1. Custody

122. The custody (in Finnish: *huolto*) of a child is a general concept, which encompasses the authority to make decisions on care, upbringing, and place of residence as well as other matters relating to the *person of a child*. The purpose of child custody is to ensure the welfare of a child. The provisions on custody of children can be found in the Child Custody and the Right of Access Act (361/1983). Instead, the concept of guardianship relates to rights and duties in relation to child's property. There is a link between the concepts of custody and guardianship as custodians of a minor act also as guardians of child's financial matters. However, the court may appoint another person to this task but this is an exception to the rule and seldom applied in practice.

The objectives of custody are to make sure that a child is taken good care of and his/her upbringing as well as supervision and protection appropriate for his or her age and stage of development are ensured (the Child Custody and the Right of Access Act, section 1). For this purpose, the person who has custody has the right to decide on the care, upbringing, place of residence and other matters relating to the person of the child (the Child Custody and the Right of Access Act, section 4). All decisions must be made in terms of the best interests of a child.

Custody ends when the child turns 18 years old or concludes marriage, whichever is earlier (the Child Custody and the Right of Access Act, section 3).

123. If the child is born in wedlock, both spouses are custody-holders by operation of the law.[113] Thus, if the mother of the child is not married at the time the child is born, she is the sole custodian. In this case the establishment of paternity at a later stage does not have any direct and automatic effect on the custody. Therefore the mother remains the sole custodian unless the parents want to exercise the custody together and to this end agree otherwise. If the parents do not live together, they usually also conclude agreements on with whom the child lives and how the other parent is to maintain contact and visit the child (*see* the Child Custody and the Right of Access Act, section 7). The local social authority may confirm the agreement between the parents. The advantage of the confirmation is that the contract on custody and residence of a child is valid and enforceable in a similar way than a final court decision. This

113. If the parents get divorced, they can agree on custody of their child. Joint custody is possible even after the divorce. If the parents cannot agree on the matter, a case may be brought to the court.

has been defined as a particular feature within Finnish system of family and child law.[114]

Custody can also be decided in a court. A child should be heard if this is possible in view of the age and stage of development of the child (the Child Custody and the Right of Access Act, section 11).

124. When the parents have joint custody, they are together responsible for the duties it brings along. As a rule, the consent of both custodians is needed when significant and important matters relating to the person of the child are decided—such as the education of the child and changes in respect the place of residence. If a parent is a sole custodian, this parent alone is able to decide matters relating to the person of the child and the consent of the other parent is not needed. Therefore, the parent who is not a custodian is not entitled to decide for example where the child is to live and reside without the consent of the parent who has sole custody. One must note though, that according to the law, the person who has custody must discuss the matter with the child, if this is possible in view of the age and stage of development of the child and the nature of the matter. The custodian is also obliged to give due consideration to the opinion and wishes of the child (the Child Custody and the Right of Access Act, section 4).

§2. Maintenance of a Child

125. Child maintenance (in Finnish: *lapsen elatus*) is a notion that is treated separately from a spousal maintenance. Provisions concerning the latter are included in the Marriage Act, whereas the former is regulated by the Child Maintenance Act (704/1975). According to it, a child has a right to be maintained by one's parents. If the child's parents live together, there is usually no need for a detailed agreement or an explicit court decision on maintenance. Thus, if the child does not live permanently with a parent or if a parent neglects to maintain a child, the parent may be ordered to pay maintenance to the child. Liability to maintain one's child is defined as a strict liability and it is not possible to renounce the right to receive maintenance on behalf of the child. Such agreements are deemed void (the Child Maintenance Act, section 7).

Parents are able to conclude a written agreement concerning the maintenance of their child. Again, the parties may request the confirmation of the agreement by the municipal social authority. By its confirmation, the agreement becomes enforceable. It means that the authority has the right to take action to enforce the collection of

114. *See* Eira Kuisma: Comparative Study on the Enforcement Procedures of Family Rights, LS/C4/2005/06, Annex 11 National Report Finland, p. 2. According to Official Statistics, in 2015, almost 50,000 agreements on child custody, right of access, and residence of children were confirmed. The agreements concerned child custody in 33,480 instances, right of access in 22,400 instances and residence in 18,170 instances. Out of child custody agreements, only 6% awarded sole custody to the mother and less than one percent to the father. *See* Statistical report 11/2016, 26 May 2016, Official Statistics of Finland, Child Maintenance and Custody, at: www.thl.fi/en/web/thlfi-en/statistics/statistics-by-topic/social-services-children-adolescents-and-families/child-maintenance-and-custody.

maintenance payments if the parent liable for payments neglects his/her duties and do not make the payments voluntarily (the Child Maintenance Act, section 8).[115] In most cases parents are able to reach an agreement and only a small part of maintenance cases ends up in a court.[116]

Note that if there is a child support agreement confirmed by the social authority or a court decision regarding child maintenance, and the parent liable for maintenance does not abide by it, the Social Insurance Institution (in Finnish: *Kansaneläkelaitos, Kela*) can pay child maintenance allowance (in Finnish: *elatustuki*). It is also payable if the amount of confirmed child support is lower than the amount of child maintenance allowance.[117]

126. The starting point for determining the proper amount of maintenance is to evaluate the needs of each child. Adequate maintenance consists of the satisfactory fulfillment of the child's material and non-material needs, proper care and education costs (the Child Maintenance Act, section 1). Another factor that affects the amount of maintenance and the content of the liability is the financial capacity of the parent under the obligation: for instance, the age, work ability, available funds, and other legal maintenance duties are taken into consideration. In addition, the child's ability and opportunities to maintain his/herself are also taken into account, as are any of those circumstances in which child maintenance does not incur any costs to the parents (the Child Maintenance Act, section 2).[118]

127. Maintenance is usually paid in cash, on a monthly basis and in advance. Parents are also free to agree otherwise. Exceptionally a maintenance payment can be determined as a lump sum (the Child Maintenance Act, section 6).[119] The amount and payment method of maintenance can be altered if the circumstances—that were taken into account when maintenance was confirmed—have notably changed. An agreement

115. For methods of collecting maintenance payments *see* Maintenance Claims—Finland, at: ec.europa.eu/civiljustice/maintenance_claim/maintenance_claim_fin_en.htm.

116. The authority may even help the parents in drawing up the agreement if they ask for assistance. In 2015, nearly 54,000 maintenance agreements were confirmed. One out of five of these included changes to existing agreements, normally reduction to the amount of maintenance. *See* Statistical report 11/2016, 26nd May 2016, Official Statistics of Finland, Child Maintenance and Custody.THL, at: www.thl.fi/en/web/thlfi-en/statistics/statistics-by-topic/social-services-children-adolescents-and-families/child-maintenance-and-custody.

117. Child maintenance allowance is also payable when there is no parent with maintenance liabilities; for instance, if the mother of the child was not married when the child was born and the paternity has not been confirmed. For more information on child maintenance allowance *see* the webpages of the Social Insurance Institution of Finland at: www.kela.fi/web/en/child-maintenance-allowance.

118. The Ministry of Justice has prepared a recommendatory instruction on the assessment of the amount of child support in 2007. It can be found at: urn.fi/URN:ISBN:978-952-466-423-3, unfortunately not in English. Even though the instruction is not legally binding, in practice it is followed; at least it is one important factor in assessing the adequacy of maintenance amount in each case.

119. A maintenance payment can also consist of movable property or real property. *See* Maintenance Claims—Finland, at: ec.europa.eu/civiljustice/maintenance_claim/maintenance_claim_fin_en.htm.

on maintenance can also be adjusted if it is considered to be unreasonable (the Child Maintenance Act, sections 11–12).[120]

A child is entitled to receive adequate maintenance from his/her parents until turning the age of 18. The maintenance obligation may even continue after this, and cover the costs incurred by education. The requirement is that it can be deemed reasonable under the circumstances (the Child Maintenance Act, section 3).

120. Due to rises in living costs, an automatic increase applies to maintenance paid periodically. The automatic increase is provided in detail by the Act on Raising Certain Maintenance Payments to Reflect Living Costs (583/2008). *See* Maintenance Claims—Finland, at: ec.europa.eu/civiljustice/maintenance_claim/maintenance_claim_fin_en.htm.

Chapter 7. Guardianship

128. If a person's (ward) mental capacity has degraded, due to illness, old age or some other comparable reason, and accordingly no longer able to take care of his/her financial interests and personal affairs, it is possible that a district court or a Local Registry Office (a guardianship authority) appoints a guardian. Appointing a guardian is also possible in cases where a person is unable to look after his/her financial interests due to absence (the Guardianship Services Act, 442/1999, section 1).[121] Appointment of a guardian is not only possible in cases where a person is incompetent, but also if the competent person needs support in managing his/her affairs. As a rule, the appointment of a guardian does not disqualify the ward from self-administering his/her property or entering into transactions (the Guardianship Services Act, section 14).

If the appointment of a guardian is not sufficient in order to safeguard the person's interests, his/her competency can be restricted. A court has a range of alternatives that can be used in these cases. A court may order that:

(1) a person may enter into given transactions or administer given property only in conjunction with the guardian;
(2) a person is not competent to enter into given transactions or to administer given property; or
(3) a person is declared incompetent.

129. It specifically reads in the Guardianship Services Act, section 18, that "no one shall be declared incompetent if the other options available are sufficient to safeguard his/her interests. Also, the competency of a person shall not otherwise be restricted more than what is necessary for the safeguarding of the interests of that person."[122]

A guardian may be a person close to the ward or alternatively a public guardian, who usually is a public official employed by a public guardianship office. A public guardian is commonly appointed if there is a conflict within the family or if a person in need of a guardian does not know anybody that would be suitable to be appointed for the task. The state is under an obligation to organize guardianship services.

130. The duties of a guardian include taking care of the ward's property and financial matters. In addition, the guardian has to protect the non-financial interests of the ward and make sure that the ward is taken care of and receives appropriate treatment.

---

121. For an English translation of the Act *see* www.finlex.fi/en/laki/kaannokset/1999/en19990442.pdf.

122. For the status of an incompetent person *see* Ch. 4 of the Guardianship Services Act. It is important to note that an incompetent person may for instance enter into transactions which, in view of the circumstances, are usual and of little significance. A person who has been declared incompetent may still decide on matters connected to his/her person, if he/she understands the significance of the matter.

The ward must have enough assets for his/her personal, everyday use (the Guardianship Services Act, section 38).[123]

131. Guardians are supervised by the Local Registry Offices and to this end the guardian must keep accounts of the ward's assets as well as his/her debts during the accounting period.[124] The guardian is not free to deal with the ward's property in any way he/she wishes. Instead, a guardian must obtain permission from the Local Registry Office for certain transactions. An authorization is required for example for conveyance or purchase of real property, taking out a loan and renouncing an inheritance (the Guardianship Services Act, section 34). In decision-making whether to grant permission or not the Local Registry Office considers the interests of the ward. As a rule, the guardian does not have the right to donate client's property (the Guardianship Services Act, section 32). The guardian is liable in damages for the loss that he/she has deliberately or negligently caused to the ward (the Guardianship Services Act, section 45).

The custodians of a minor child also act as ipso iure guardians and accordingly they are responsible for the administration of the child's property. It is, thus, possible that a special guardian has been appointed for the task (the Guardianship Services Act, section 4).

If a child does not have a special property, guardianship can be a quite effortless task for the parents. However, if a child receives significant assets, or if the child becomes an heir, the actions of the parents (or in exceptional cases other custodians) in the administration of the child's property are supervised by the Local Registry Office. In such cases, supervision happens by means of accountability. The guardianship of the child is also entered into a register of guardianship affairs, maintained by a Local Registry Office (the Guardianship Services Act, sections 65–66).

132. The Act on Continuing Powers of Attorney (648/2007) came into force in 2007. The law provides means by which a person may—within his/her right to self-determination—make preparations for becoming functionally incapable to handle his/her financial affairs.[125] Accordingly, a person may issue a continuing power of attorney. It is a deed in writing in which a donor appoints a donee.[126] In the deed the donor may define the scope of the power of attorney. The donor is able to authorize the donee to deal with matters regarding the management of the property and other financial matters. The authorization may also cover the non-financial domain, including personal matters. The power of attorney may be general or it can cover only a certain task specified in the deed.

123. *See* the webpages of the Judicial Administration at: oikeus.fi/edunvalvonta/en/index/hakeminen/dutiesofaguardian.html and the webpages of the International Guardianship Network at: www.international-guardianship.com/pdf/GBC/GBC_Finland.pdf.

124. Within three months of the commencement of his/her duties, the guardian must provide the Local Registry Office with an inventory of the assets and liabilities of the ward that are to be managed by the guardian (the Guardianship Services Act, s. 48). The guardian must regularly, usually once a year, provide a Local Registry Office with a statement of accounts (the Guardianship Services Act, s. 51).

125. Council of Europe: Principles Concerning Continuing Powers of Attorney and Advance Directives for Incapacity. Council of Europe Publishing 2009, p. 21.

126. As a starting point, any person may act as a donee if he/she is willing for the task. However, when confirming the document a Local Registry Office have to make sure that a donee is suitable. For instance, a person with limited competency cannot act as a donee.

The continuing power of attorney comes into force if the donor becomes incapable of managing his or her affairs and the donee applies for a confirmation of the deed at the Local Registry Office. The donee has to provide the Registry Office with the original power of attorney and a medical certificate stating that the donor has become incapable of managing his/her affairs that are covered by the power of attorney. The power of attorney comes into force on confirmation by the Local Registry Office. The donee is also supervised by the Registry Office.[127]

127. For measures to protect the donor from misuse of power, *see* the webpages of Alzheimer Europe, country comparisons at: www.alzheimer-europe.org/Policy-in-Practice2/Country-comparisons/2010-Legal-capacity-and-proxy-decision-making/Finland.

Part III. Matrimonial Property Law

Chapter 1. Rights and Obligations of Spouses

§1. General Principles

133. Through the lenses of property law the married spouses are viewed as two individuals, not dependent on each other. Therefore transactions and conveyances between them have the same legal consequences as if they were not married to each other. A personal relationship between the parties does not as such, as a rule, affect the ownership of property. Property belonging to a spouse upon the conclusion of the marriage will remain his/her also during the marriage. The same rule applies to property that a spouse acquires during the marriage or receives as an inheritance or a gift. It belongs solely to the title-holding spouse.

The spouses can acquire property together. The co-ownership is, thus, not created by marriage; instead, it is created according to the principles of property law and therefore by a common intention of owning property together. The presumption of co-ownership does not apply if it is proven by the other spouse that the title of property belongs to him or her only. With regard to movable property, a special provision in the Marriage Act, section 89, creates presumed co-ownership but only if it cannot be established which of the spouses is the title-holder. The provision is applicable in the separation of property of the spouses. Moreover, according to the Marriage Act, section 65, necessary items that a spouse has acquired for his or her personal use with funds given by the other spouse under the maintenance obligation belongs to the first-mentioned spouse.

134. With regard to immovable property, general rules of property law apply. Again, if the title of the property is registered to both spouses, it creates a strong presumption as who owns the property. The presumption is rebuttable if the intention was—at the time of the conveyance—that the property belongs to one of the spouses only. Vice versa, even though the other spouse has the title alone, it can be deemed that the property was meant to be common property.

In precedents involving the ownership (KKO 1988:85 and KKO 2016:37), the Supreme Court has confirmed that the intention of the parties—at the moment when the property was acquired—is decisive. The common intention is construed in view of all the facts and circumstances of each case: who has the title of property, who has funded its acquisition, who has the building permit, who has taken care of repayment of a loan, who has worked at the construction site etc.

§2. The Household Expenses

135. The spouses have a duty to participate in the common household of the family and the maintenance of the spouses to the best of each of their abilities (the Marriage Act, section 46). This includes the fulfillment of the personal needs of each spouse and the common needs of the spouses. The duty can be fulfilled in various ways, for example by doing household work or by giving funds to cover expenses rising from the common household.[128] Because of the duty of maintaining the family, there is an exception to the rule that each spouse is solely liable for a debt that he/she has incurred. According to the Marriage Act, section 52, spouses are jointly and severally liable for debts incurred by one of them for the purpose of maintaining the family. However, a monetary loan is never deemed to be a household debt under the above-mentioned provision.

The duty to participate in the common household and the duty to maintain the other spouse are not connected to the fact how matrimonial property relations are organized between the spouses. Instead, maintenance is considered to be a strict, personal duty arising from the marriage. Therefore, the duty cannot be limited or abrogated even by concluding a marital settlement, as the existence of the duty is not bound with the existence of a marital right between spouses.

The maintenance of children is regulated separately, in the Act on Child Maintenance.

§3. The Matrimonial Home

136. In marriage both spouses have, as a rule, the status of full-fledged owners where their property relations are concerned. Thus, the marital bond restricts owner's rights with regard to property in whose use each spouse has a strong interest. Restrictions on the administration of property have a protective function, rooted in social considerations and apply to the property specifically mentioned in the Marriage Act, sections 38–39. The common home of the spouses,[129] the movable property that forms household goods in the family home, tools used by a spouse and movable property personally used by

128. Since a housework is deemed to be a fulfillment of a maintenance, a spouse is not expected to be compensated for this work done at home, *see* Kirsti Kurki-Suonio: National Report: Property Relationship Between Spouses – Finland. Commission on European Family Law: Country Reports, 2008, p. 6.

129. The restrictions on the conveyance apply both to a real estate and to a flat. The latter is considered as movable property in Finland.

a spouse or the children are protected by these provisions.[130] The idea behind the regulation is that property important to the family is protected and remains available to its members also when this property belongs solely to one spouse.[131]

Under the provisions on restrictions, the owner of the matrimonial home cannot sell the property without the other spouse consenting to it. The permission must be in writing.[132] Naturally, the consent is also needed also when for example spouses own property in common and one of them wants to convey his/her share to a third party.

The permission of the other spouse is not necessary, if the property to be conveyed is mainly intended for some other use as a common home of the spouses. Therefore, it is important to define the nature of the property in question.[133]

137. The system protects property during the marriage irrespective whether there is actual need for the protection and accordingly, discretion of individual circumstances is not allowed. In this sense the protection under the provisions can be deemed as an automatic and a quite harsh from the perspective of the owner. In addition, the provisions on restrictions on the administration of property are not connected to a marital right and the system cannot be eroded by concluding a marital settlement in where the spouses remove the property in question from the scope of the marital right.

Regarding the written consent of the spouse, contractual freedom is limited to protect a spouse, as he/she cannot waive (in a legally valid way) his/her right in advance and before the actual circumstances of the transaction are known. A conveyance entered into by a spouse without a valid consent of the other spouse can be declared void, if the other spouse claims it in a court. This has to be done within three months of he/she becoming aware of the conveyance.[134]

§4. Transactions Between Spouses

138. During marriage each spouse owns his/her property and also debts remain separate. Under the separation of property each is able to manage his/her property independently. In addition, according to the Marriage Act, section 33, spouses are free to conclude agreements and enter into mutual transactions. They have contractual freedom *inter partes,* as well as *ultra partes.*

130. Provisions on household goods, tools and movables for personal use have been described practically desuetudo because they are very seldom claimed to. *See* Eva Gottberg: Study on Matrimonial Property Regimes and the Property of Unmarried Couples in Private International Law and internal Law. National Report: Finland. Commission Européenne JAI/A3/2001/03, p. 9.

131. *See* the webpages of the Judicial Administration at: oikeus.fi/en/index/esitteet/avioliittolaki/puolisoidenoikeudetjavelvollisuudetavioliitossa.html.

132. Restrictions protect the use of the property and therefore the establishment of right of use is deemed to correspond to a conveyance.

133. If a spouse refuses to give a consent or obtaining it is for some other reason impossible, the district court may, upon petition, to grant permission to a conveyance or to another transaction.

134. Thus, protection may be given to an acquirer of immovable property under certain circumstances. Requirements include that the acquirer has acted in good faith and the title of the acquirer has been registered. It is also possible that the transfer of movable property gains validity even though the permission of the other spouse is lacking. *See* in detail the Marriage Act, s. 39.

A spouse may donate property to the other spouse[135] and gifts are valid without any special measures to be taken by them (if movable property). Thus, in order to gain protection against third parties (such as creditors of the donor) one must notify the donation of movable property to the Local Registry Office. A separate notification is not necessary in case a donation is referred to in a registered marital settlement (the Marriage Act, section 45). If a spouse donates immovable property to the other spouse, the general rules on conveyance of real property are applicable in order to gain validity between the parties. As the conveyance is registered under these rules, no additional measures (in order to gain protection against third parties) are necessary.[136]

Spouses may also conclude an employment contract between them in which case the rules of labor law are applicable. Instead, if no agreement was made and the spouse who has assisted the other spouse in the latter's business wants to receive compensation, he/she has to prove that compensation was meant to be paid, or that its payment, with a view to the nature of the work and the other circumstances, is reasonable. It is possible to claim compensation in a court, but an action is time-barred and has to be brought within a year from the end of the calendar year during which the work was performed. Compensation paid thereafter is deemed as a gift (the Marriage Act, section 64).

135. Gifts between spouses were not valid (except for usual gifts of reasonable value) until 1992. The prohibition was repealed when the Act of Recovery of Assets to a Bankruptcy Estate (758/1991) came into force. *See* Eva Gottberg: Study on the Matrimonial Property Regimes and the Property of Unmarried Couples in Private International Law and Internal Law. National Report: Finland. Commission Européenne JAI/A3/2001/03, p. 15.

136. *See* the Code of Real Estate (540/1995), in English at: http://www.finlex.fi/fi/laki/kaannokset/1995/en19950540.pdf.

Chapter 2. Agreements and Matrimonial Property

§1. The Marriage Settlement

139. The statutory regime governing matrimonial property relations between spouses is based on the marital right (in Finnish: *avio-oikeus*). The regime is, thus, an elective one. Spouses may conclude agreements through which they alter their statutory legal rights and relations in respect of matrimonial property.

The engaged persons can, either at any time before the marriage or during the marriage, conclude a marriage settlement (in Finnish: *avioehto*, the Marriage Act, section 41) that is registered with the Local Registry Office (the Marriage Act, sections 44 and 66).[137] In order to gain legal effects, the registration of the settlement has to take place before divorce proceedings are initiated in a court.[138] The matrimonial property regime can also be changed during the marriage. Changes cannot be made by one spouse alone if the other spouse does not agree. Only exception in this respect is the other spouse's personal bankruptcy (the Marriage Act, section 35).

140. In a marriage settlement, any property that is owned or later acquired by the spouses can be excluded from the sphere of a marital right. If the agreement is comprehensive and covers all of the property of the spouses, then upon the dissolution of the marriage their property is not divided based on the marital right. Instead, property is separated and each spouse keeps what he/she owns.

Thus, the contractual freedom of the spouses entrenches also to the marriage settlement to a certain respect. The settlement does not have to be comprehensive and it is possible to stipulate in it that a spouse has no matrimonial right to certain property belonging to the other spouse, such as inherited property. The marriage settlement may also be one-sided, excluding the marital right of one of the spouses only.

There are strict requirements of form (the Marriage Act, section 42). The marriage settlement has to be concluded in writing and it must be dated and signed. In addition, there should be two witnesses. They should be impartial and disinterested, without any close connections to the spouses (the Marriage Act, section 66).

141. A marriage settlement affects the distribution of matrimonial assets when the marriage is dissolved either on the death of a spouse or on divorce. However, a settlement is not necessarily binding. Its terms can be derogated from, or it can be set aside altogether in the distribution of matrimonial property in cases where compliance with the marriage settlement would lead to an unreasonable result. It is also noteworthy, that an examination of the agreement's validity is not carried out by an authority when

137. Pursuant to s. 42 of the Marriage Act in case a spouse is not entitled to make a marital agreement himself/herself due to legal incapacity or a restriction of legal capacity, he/she must acquire a written approval from his/her guardian for it.

138. There is a register for matrimonial matters. The Local Registry Office functions as the register authority. *See* more at: www.coupleseurope.eu/en/finland/topics/4-can-or-must-the-matrimonial-property-regime-be-registered/.

its registration is applied for. The spouse's right to appeal to a latent formal error is not time-barred.

In legal literature it has been unanimously stated that the spouses cannot connect the legal effects of their settlement with the cause of dissolution of the marriage. In practice this interpretation has been contested and not coherently followed. The interpretational problem was partially settled by the Supreme Court in its decision KKO 2000:100. In this case there was a marriage settlement that gave the marital right for spouses only if the marriage was dissolved by death. The agreement excluded the marital right in case of divorce. The Supreme Court decided that the agreement was valid. This decision has, however, been discussed and criticized in legal literature as being against the clear wording of the law. In practice it is followed, though.[139]

§2. The Marital Agreement

142. Spouses may also make a marital agreement (divorce contract, in Finnish: *sopimus avioeron varalta*) governing what happens in the event of a divorce and thus decide how the matrimonial property (or part of it) is distributed. These contracts can handle the distribution of assets upon divorce and regulate in detail when and how compensation—including maintenance—to the other spouse is payable. The ambit of marital agreement is not restricted, unlike that of marriage settlement, which can only regulate the spouses' marital rights to each other's property. In practice, if there is a conflict between contents of a marriage settlement and a marital agreement, the latter can render the effects of a marriage settlement void (in *inter partes* –relations).

Because there are no provisions concerning a marital agreement in the Marriage Act, its justification lies on the spouses' freedom of contract (the Marriage Act, section 33). In addition, the effectiveness of the agreement is assessed according to the law of obligations and therefore it is possible to challenge the agreement for instance on grounds pertaining to the invalidity of legal transactions if the agreement is deemed to be unreasonable.[140]

143. The agreement is free in form and may contain any terms whatsoever regarding the distribution of property in case of divorce. It can even cover terms that are personal by nature. In this regard the marital agreement differs from a marriage settlement, whose form and content are regulated in detail by the provisions of the Marriage Act. Moreover, a marital agreement is not affected by time limits and it can be effectively made before concluding a marriage and during it. It is not required that the breakdown of the marriage has to be foreseeable at the time the marital agreement is concluded. Since there are no time constraints, a marital agreement can be made even when divorce proceedings are pending. The only time limit is that the agreement must be made before the distribution of marital assets has taken place. The marital agreement binds also the estate distributor whom the court appoints to carry out the distribution of the spouses' property.

139. Hilkka Salmenkylä: Finland. In: J. Stewart (ed.): Family Law – Jurisdictional Comparisons 2013. Thomson Reuters 2013, p. 186.

140. The Contracts Act (228/1929), s. 36, available in English at: www.finlex.fi/en/laki/kaannokset/1929/en19290228.pdf.

Chapter 3. The Legal Matrimonial Regime

§1. General

144. Under the provisions of the Marriage Act, the default matrimonial regime is the one where each spouse has a *marital right* to all of the property of the other spouse (the Marriage Act, section 35). A marital right does not have legal effects as long as the marriage lasts. It is applied in the distribution of the marital property relations between spouses upon divorce or the death of the other spouse (in Finnish: *ositus*). However, the legal regime that is built on matrimonial right is optional. The spouses may alter the regime by concluding a marital settlement. In case both spouses have through the marriage settlement excluded their marital rights, their property is separated upon dissolution of the marriage (in Finnish: *erottelu*).

According to the rules of private international law, spouses have a limited right to opt for another matrimonial property system in cases their marriage has legally relevant connections to foreign legal systems. In this way they can change the applicable legal regime between them. Thus, contractual freedom is limited in this respect. They are entitled to choose either the law of the state where one spouse or both spouses are domiciled or whose citizen a spouse is at the time of the agreement. If the domicile of one or both spouses has moved to another state during the marriage, also the law of the state where both spouses last were domiciled may be chosen as the applicable law (the Marriage Act, section 130).[141]

§2. The Relevant Dates

145. A distribution of matrimonial property can be made when the marriage has been dissolved by death of the other spouse or proceedings concerning divorce is pending in a court. In a latter case the decisive time point is when the application by a spouse or both spouses has been lodged in a court. If a property is transferred from a spouse to another spouse before this date, it is not deemed as dissolution of the matrimonial regime—instead, normal rules of property and tax law apply.

Everything that a spouse owns at the time of death of either spouse or when a divorce application is lodged in a court, is in the scope of matrimonial right. Therefore, a spouse has no marital right to property that the other spouse has earned, inherited or received as a gift after court proceedings for divorce have been instituted (the Marriage Act, section 90).

146. Property is subject to the marital right of the other spouse if the divorce proceedings have lapsed for another reason than the death of the other spouse during

141. Note that Council Regulation (EU) 2016/1103 of Jun. 24, 2016 implementing enhanced cooperation in the area of jurisdiction, applicable law and the recognition and enforcement of decisions in matters of matrimonial property regimes will be applicable also in Finland from Jan. 29, 2019.

their pendency (the Marriage Act, section 90). In other words, if the divorce lapses and the distribution of the matrimonial regime has not taken place, the commencement of the divorce proceedings has no legal effect to the marital regime or property relations between spouses. Everything continues normally in terms of financial affairs.

147. Nevertheless, it is possible that a divorce lapses and the spouses decide to continue their marriage, even though a distribution of assets has taken place. In these cases distribution is valid and enforceable. After the distribution, thus, neither spouse has a marital right to the property of the other spouse, unless they state otherwise in a marriage settlement concluded after the distribution (the Marriage Act, section 107).

§3. Valuation of Assets In the Distribution

148. The marital right entitles the spouse to one half of the net value of all of the spouses' property subject to the right. To this end, the property has to be inventoried and valued. Nowadays it is common that each spouse has many kinds of assets, including for instance real estate, bank accounts, art, antiques collections, life and pension insurances, etc. As the portfolios can be fairly complex, a question of their valuation can be a point of contention in a distribution of marital assets.

If spouses can agree on the valuation of property – even partially – also the estate distributor is bound by their agreement. In case the agreement is not reached, the value of the property is determined on the date of the distribution.

§4. Who Carries Out the Distribution

149. When divorce proceedings are pending or a spouse has died, either party may demand the distribution or separation of the matrimonial assets. Distribution can be made by an agreement.[142] In addition, as the distribution is not mandatory, spouses may even decide not to go through with it. However, the right to demand the distribution is not time-barred. If spouses decide not to make any distribution, it would therefore be sensible to make an agreement which states that either spouse has taken what is his/her, and that there is no further demands. Without such an agreement, it is possible to demand a distribution even after twenty years following the divorce (as in a Supreme Court case KKO 2001:56). The distribution may be demanded even when the ex-spouse has remarried.

If the parties cannot agree on the distribution of the matrimonial assets by themselves, it can be made officially, by a court-appointed distributor.[143] Normally, the distributor establishes an inventory in order to list the assets covered by the marital right and the assets separated from it. The inventory of the assets and debts of the spouses is the foundation of the distribution. The distributor is not free in his/her discretion as the Marriage Act gives quite specific guidance according to which the

142. In case a marriage ends to the death of the other spouse, the distribution is made between a widow and the parties to the estate of the deceased spouse.

143. In practice most distributions are carried out by an agreement of the spouses. There are approximately 14,000 divorces per year but less than 1,000 distributors are appointed.

distribution has to be made. The distributor is also bound by agreements concluded by the spouses either before the commencement of the distribution or after it. In fact, the distributor is in all cases obliged to strive for an amicable end-result and an agreement between the parties involved.

150. The distributor's powers and duties are quite extensive as he/she ascertains the validity of the agreements made between the parties during marriage—including a marriage settlement and a marital agreement. The distributor is also entitled (and obliged) to decide contentious property issues between spouses. Determination of ownership follows the principles of civil law, except for cases where it cannot be proven which spouse owns certain movable object. Pursuant to the Marriage Act, section 89, the spouses are then deemed to have acquired it jointly and with equal rights.

After the calculation and valuation of the net assets of each spouse, the spouse that owns more, have to give his/her property (in the ambit of marital right) or a corresponding amount of money to the other spouse (in Finnish: *tasinko*), so that the shares of each are equal. The spouse who is obliged to hand over property to the other spouse, may decide what to give in order to equalize the final shares. An estate distributor is not able to intervene if the property the owner has decided to hand over has value in recipient's hand.

151. If the spouses agree themselves on how to distribute the matrimonial property, they should make a signed deed of distribution. Two witnesses are required in order to affirm that the signatures of the spouses are authentic. When the distributor has been appointed, he/she signs the deed of distribution even if the deed is based partially or fully on the agreement of the spouses. No witnesses are required.

If a spouse is not happy with a distribution made by an estate distributor, he/she can contest it by bringing an action against the other spouse in a district court within six months of the date of the distribution.[144]

§5. Deferred Community System

152. As described above, each spouse owns his or her property during marriage and is free to dispose of it without the consent of the other spouse. Thus, each spouse has a marital right to the property of the other spouse in case they have no marital settlement stating otherwise. Under the marital right, the surviving spouse (in the case of death) and the heirs of the deceased spouse or each of the spouses (in the case of divorce) acquire half of the net property of the spouses upon the distribution of the marital property (section 35 of the Marriage Act). Net property is each spouse's property after his or her debts have been deducted.[145] At the distribution of matrimonial property the party that has to hand over property to the other spouse may decide what to give. However, the property conveyed to the other party has to be marital—not separate—

144. According to legal literature, in practice it is not common to contest distributions of matrimonial property. *See*, i.e., Hilkka Salmenkylä: Finland. In: J. Stewart (ed.): Family Law – Jurisdictional Comparisons 2013. Thomson Reuters 2013, p. 189.

145. Kirsti Kurki-Suonio: Property Relationship Between Spouses – Finland. Commission on European Family Law: Country Reports, 2008, p. 11.

property. Instead of property, money may be given to the value determined for the property at the distribution.

153. A spouse may also own separate property that is not included in the distribution of matrimonial assets. Even though spouses have not decided to limit marital right's legal effects by concluding a marriage settlement (or a marital agreement), there still can exist separate property that is excluded from the marital right under the provisions of the Marriage Act. A donor of a gift or a testator can exclude the marital right of the spouse of a donee or a beneficiary to property received as a gift or due to a will. In addition, a policyholder can determine that the spouse of an insurance beneficiary has no marital right to such property which his/her spouse has received based on a beneficiary clause of an insurance (the Marriage Act, section 35). Without such stipulation excluding the marital right, property acquired, for instance as a gift, belongs to the scope of marital right if it is given or received before divorce is pending in a court or marriage has ended to the death of a spouse.

Property can also be outside the scope of a marital right if it can be determined to be personal by nature. Section 35 of the Marriage Act states that "The provisions on marital right shall apply to a right which cannot be conveyed or which otherwise is of a personal nature only when this is not in contradiction with any specific provisions on such a right." For instance copyrights and legal pension rights are deemed to be personal and therefore outside the scope of marital right.

154. The Marriage Act includes a provision that underlines the personal nature of the marital right; namely, the right does not pass to creditors of a spouse and accordingly, if the property of a spouse is surrendered into bankruptcy, the other spouse is not obliged to hand over any of his/her property in the distribution of matrimonial property (the Marriage Act, section 103.2).

Marital right does not have effects during a marriage since each spouse has a right to administer his or her property freely and independently, without the consent of the other spouse. Exceptions to this rule concern only transactions of the family home and movable property used in a common household, necessary tools used by the other spouse and movable property which is meant for the personal use of the other spouse or the children (the Marriage Act, sections 37–39). It is noteworthy, thus, that the scope of these restrictions is not affected by excluding the marital right by a marital settlement.

155. Even though the marital right does not affect owner's position during a marriage, according to the section 37 of the Marriage Act property subject to the marital right of the other spouse should be administered in a way that it does not unnecessarily decrease to the detriment of the other spouse. As said, this provision does not give the other spouse rights to prevent the owner from conveying his or her property subject to the marital right as long as the marriage lasts. Therefore interventions to transactions are not possible. However, a conveyance that has decreased the value of the property and therefore decreased the matrimonial rights of the other spouse can be taken into account in the dissolution of the marriage. The other spouse has a right to be compensated in the distribution, if it can be proven that the other spouse has by mismanaging his or her financial affairs unnecessarily decreased property subject to marital right.[146]

146. Kirsti Kurki-Suonio: Property Relationship Between Spouses – Finland. Commission on European Family Law: Country Reports, 2008, p. 18.

Compensation is, thus, payable only in exceptionally as only transactions that are inappropriate in respect of the circumstances at the time of the transactions, can be considered to give the right to compensation.[147]

If a spouse or both of them lack net property after their debts have been covered, the marital right does not have any practical meaning as a spouse without net property does not have to give anything to the other spouse in the distribution. Creditors have a priority over the spouse or the heirs of the spouse. If a marriage is dissolved by a death of a spouse, the distribution between the parties have to be made before the assets of the estate can be divided between the heirs. In other words, a spouse always has a priority over the heirs.

§6. Separation of Property

156. In case both spouses have mutually excluded a marital right, their property is separated upon dissolution of the marriage. Accordingly, each spouse is entitled to property that he/she owns.

It is possible that spouses are not able to carry out the separation by an agreement. Therefore a spouse it entitled to apply for an estate distributor to carry out the separation. The distributor is entitled to resolve the contentious property issues between the spouses.

If a spouse is not happy with a separation made by an estate distributor, he/she can contest it by bringing an action against the other spouse in a district court within six months of the date of the separation.

§7. Preferential Rights over Specific Property

157. Before the distribution of matrimonial property, a spouse has the right first to take clothes and other articles belonging to him/her if meant for his or her personal use only. However, the right is limited as a spouse is not able to take more than what can be deemed reasonable. Definition of reasonableness is dependent on the circumstances of the spouses (the Marriage Act, section 91).

When the distribution of matrimonial property follows the death of a spouse and the value of the property to be distributed is small, the surviving spouse has additional right to certain movables. The right covers the necessary household goods and tools and other movables he or she needs in order to carry on his or her business. A widow enjoys the right even if the heirs of the other spouse do not therefore receive whole of the property what they otherwise would be entitled to in the distribution (the Marriage Act, section 103).

147. Eva Gottberg: Study on Matrimonial Property Regimes and the Property of Unmarried Couples in Private International Law and Internal Law. National Report: Finland. Commission Européenne JAI/A3/2001/03, p. 14.

§8. Adjustment of the Distribution

158. If the other spouse (or heirs of the deceased spouse) is in the opinion that the end-result of the distribution would not be justifiable and equitable under the circumstances, he/she may demand an adjustment (in Finnish: *sovittelu*). If the demand is accepted, the rules normally applicable to a distribution of property (also in cases of separation) can be derogated from. An adjustment should be applied only in exceptional cases and requirements for it are specifically outlined in the Marriage Act, section 103.b.

In general, a spouse that claims that there are reasons to adjust the distribution has to show that it would otherwise lead to an unreasonable result or to the other spouse receiving unjust financial benefit. Consideration has to be based on different factors, such as the duration of the marriage, the activities of the spouses for their common household and for the accumulation and preservation of the property. It is also possible to take account other comparable facts regarding the finances and the common household of the spouses.

159. There is also a provision in the Marriage Act on how the adjustment can be carried out and what can be ordered. Firstly, it is possible to rule that a spouse does not receive any property under the marital right. It is also possible to leave certain property or part of property outside the scope of marital right. This property can be either that which the spouse has got while the spouses were living separated or which the spouse had at the time of conclusion of a marriage. In addition, property that the spouse has received during the marriage as an inheritance, a donation or as a beneficiary under a will can be totally or partly excluded from the marital right. The adjustment may also extend to a marriage settlement; in other words, if a marital right has been restricted by a settlement, the adjustment may lead to an end-result where the excluded property is considered as property subject to a marital right.[148]

If property is not subject to marital right based on a stipulation of a third party (in respect to a gift or a will), the stipulation cannot be adjusted.

The adjustment of the distribution of matrimonial property may be claimed at the distribution or even after it. If it is claimed after the distribution has been carried out, the rules on contesting a distribution apply.

§9. Distribution of Matrimonial Property and Third Parties

160. The freedom of spouses to contract covers the distribution and accordingly spouses may agree over the distribution as they wish. The rules of the distribution stipulated in the Marriage Act, as such, do not have to be followed. The other spouse may hand over more or less property than what he/she is obliged to. Since conveyances and transactions connected to the distribution may be improper from the perspective

148. If spouses have concluded a marriage agreement concerning the distribution, the requirements for its adjustment are laid down in the contract law. Thus, the requirements for adjusting the agreement should be in accordance with the preconditions for adjustment that are included in s. 103.b of the Marriage Act.

of third parties (such as creditors), there is a rule in the Marriage Act to ensure that the rights of for instance debtors are not jeopardized.

If, in the distribution of matrimonial property, a spouse has handed over property to the other spouse to an amount considerably exceeding what he/she should have handed over according to the law, the distribution may be reversed into a bankruptcy estate—in accordance with the provisions in the Act on the Recovery of Assets into a Bankruptcy Estate (the Marriage Act, section 104). Thus, the section does not apply if the amount is less than what should have been handed over according to the provisions on distribution of matrimonial property.

Part IV. Succession Law

Chapter 1. Introduction

161. The foundation for intestate and testamentary succession is laid down in one single act, namely the Code of Inheritance (40/1965, in Finnish: *perintökaari*). The Code includes twenty-six chapters. It covers provisions on procedure of the inheritance, and also provisions on to whom and how the estate is distributed. The Code has been amended on many occasions after it came into force and especially in respect to the position of the surviving spouse.

The estate administration and distribution is naturally connected to several other areas of law and thus, the Code of Inheritance cannot be applied—or the estate distributed—without taking into account, for instance, property and contract legislation, guardianship law, and tax laws. Matters involving estates are also connected to the child law.

Matrimonial property and inheritance are intertwined with each other, often in a quite complicated way. If the deceased was or had been married—and was also survived by lineal descendants—the matrimonial property regime has to be dissolved or the property of the spouses separated in order to clarify and realize the estate. In addition, a position of a surviving spouse is protected under certain measures adopted in the matrimonial property and inheritance law.

Chapter 2. Intestate Succession

§1. The Opening of the Succession

I. General

162. The death commences a process in which the estate is settled and finally distributed to the heirs of a deceased. It is only in the distribution when the ownership of property is transferred to a beneficiary (an heir or a beneficiary under a will). It is noteworthy that the principle of universal succession is not applicable and therefore property rights and debts of the deceased person do not devolve as such to his/her successors upon death.

II. Estate Inventory

163. Even though authorities are not actively involved in any of the proceedings in relation to an estate, drawing up an estate inventory deed is obligatory if the deceased was domiciled in Finland. The estate inventory deed (in Finnish: *perukirja*) is a document where the standing of the estate is accounted for. Everybody having an interest in the estate has to be listed in the inventory,[149] as well as all the assets and liabilities of the deceased. The property is also valued in the inventory. If the deceased left a widow, also the surviving spouse's assets and debts—and their valuation—are included in the inventory.[150]

164. The inventory deed of the deceased's estate serves several purposes. As inheritance tax is payable a deed serves as a tax return for estate taxation purposes.[151] The Local Registry Office may also upon application supplement an inventory deed by a separate certificate of its public standing, stating that the list of the heirs and beneficiaries is accurate and true (the Code of Inheritance, Chapter 20, sections 9a–c). After the confirmation the deed can be used as a proof of the position as an heir or a beneficiary under a will. The inventory deed is also a basis for further acts in order to settle and distribute the estate.

---

149. The inventory has to include an extract from the population records, in order to ascertain the legal heirs. An extract can be obtained from the Local Registry Office or parish office. *See* i.e., the website of Financial Supervisory Authority at: www.finanssivalvonta.fi/en/Financial_customer/Contacts/Estate/Agreements/Pages/Default.aspx.

150. For more detailed information on what data should be disclosed to the estate inventory, *see* the webpages of Tax Administration at: www.vero.fi/en/individuals/property/inheritance/estate_inventory_meeting_and_estate_inv/.

151. A tax on inheritance is imposed on the individual share of each beneficiary. The level of tax depends on the kinship between the deceased and the heir, *see* the webpages of Tax Administration at: https://www.vero.fi/en/individuals/property/inheritance/.

The duty to organize an estate inventory meeting and to carry out an estate inventory lies primarily on the one who is handling the property of the estate and who therefore is considered to be best informed of the deceased person's financial matters and property. Usually, this person is a widow or a close relative, normally a child of the deceased.

The estate inventory has to be completed within three months after the date of death. It is, however, possible to request an extension of a deadline on the basis of the nature of the estate or other special reasons (the Code of Inheritance, Chapter 20, section 1). The inventory has to be sent to the Tax Administration within one month after completing it. If the estate inventory is not drawn up in time, this may cause detrimental effects, for instance, raised inheritance tax.

III. Missing Persons and Absentees

165. If somebody is missing, he/she may be declared dead by a decision of a district court of the last known habitual residence of him/her. Submitting a petition for a declaration is possible even immediately after a person has been gone missing if at the time of the disappearance the person was in an accident causing immediate mortal danger. Another option is that a petition is submitted after a waiting period; the length of a time that has to be waited varies from one to five years depending on the circumstances of the case. There is no deadline in making an application for a declaration of death.

The declaration creates a presumption of death and of the moment of death (the Act on Declaration of Death (127/2005), section 11).

§2. The Heirs

I. Capacity to Succeed and Renunciation of the Inheritance

166. A person is able to inherit the deceased if he or she is alive at the moment of the deceased's death. An exception in this respect is a child conceived before this if the child is later born alive (the Code of Inheritance, Chapter 1, section 1).

According to the provisions under the Code of Inheritance, the right to inherit requires a legally valid relationship between the deceased and the heir; for example, a relationship between the parent and the child. Under the provisions of the child law, it is possible to confirm the paternity even after the deceased's death (the Paternity Act, section 67). Also in these cases a child has a right of inheritance. If an estate distribution has taken place before the establishment of paternity, a child may request rectification of an estate distribution (in Finnish: *perinnönjaon oikaisu*). The provisions in Chapter 23a of the Code of Inheritance apply to rectification of an estate distribution and the duty to return property to the estate.

167. Contracts pertaining to the estate of a person still alive are not valid. As a consequence, a person cannot dispose of his or her assets by contractual means *mortis causa*. Hence, an heir may unilaterally renounce his/her right to the estate either before or after the death of a deceased. The renunciation is valid if an heir accepts the will or in some other way in writing notifies the deceased that he/she renounces the inheritance. However, if the heir included in the first parentela has not received reasonable consideration at the time of renunciation, he/she is entitled to his/her forced portion. This right does not exist if a spouse of the heir, on the basis of a will, or his / her descendants, by operation of law or on the basis of a will, receive property corresponding to the forced portion (the Code of Inheritance, Chapter 17, section 1).

A renunciation can also take place after the deceased has died. Accordingly, an heir or a beneficiary under a will is able to renounce his/her right at this stage but the requirement is that he/she has not taken part in the administration of the estate—or otherwise taken such measures which indicate to a third person that a heir/beneficiary has accepted and received the inheritance or the will (the Code of Inheritance, Chapter 17, section 2a).

168. An heir has to enforce the inheritance right within ten years of the deceased's death, otherwise he/she loses his/her right to inherit (the statute of limitation, Chapter 16 of the Code of Inheritance). The same rule applies to a beneficiary under a will. However, if the right under a will begins at a later date, the right has to be enforced within ten years of the said later date. It is possible, thus, that a person, who has a right to the estate in addition to or immediately following an heir or a beneficiary under a testament, petitions that the court orders that the said person is to enforce his or her right within a given, shorter period of time. This period cannot exceed one year, after the date when the person in question was informed of the disposition.

If an heir has lost his or her right to inherit under the statute of limitation, the inheritance devolves on the person who would have received it if the heir had died before the deceased (the Code of Inheritance, Chapter 16, section 3).

II. Commorientes

169. Sometimes it is not certain whether a person was alive at the moment when the deceased died and there is a presumption applicable in these cases. Pursuant to the Code of Inheritance, Chapter 1, section 2, if an heir has died and it cannot be proven that he/she survived the deceased, it is presumed that the heir died before the deceased.

III. Unworthiness to Succeed

170. Only under certain exceptional circumstances—stipulated in detail in the Code of Inheritance—the deceased may disinherit an heir. Disinheritance is restricted to cases where the heir, through a deliberate act, has seriously offended the deceased or his/her close relatives. In addition, if the heir has continuously acted immorally, there is a possibility of disinheritance (the Code of Inheritance, Chapter 15, section 4). Validly disinherited heir has no right to a forced portion.

It is also possible to disinherit a surviving spouse. The disinheritance of a widow means that he/she loses a right to keep the estate property in his/her possession according to the Chapter 3 of the Inheritance Code.

171. The disinheritance has to be done in a certain form; in other words, in a will in order to gain legal effect. The testator has to state and explain in a will what are the reasons for which his/her decision of disinheritance is based (the Code of Inheritance, Chapter 15, section 4). In case of a legally valid disinheritance, an inheritance devolves on the person who would have been entitled to the inheritance if the heir had died before the deceased (the Code of Inheritance, Chapter 15, section 5).

In addition to the above-mentioned cases, it is possible that a person loses his/her inheritance rights in case he or she has deliberately destroyed or concealed the testament of the testator. These cases require courts' involvement, though, as the court decides whether a person has forfeited his or her right to inherit or receive under a will at the death of the deceased. The right can be forfeited in full or only partly (the Code of Inheritance, Chapter 15, section 4).

IV. The Anomalous Succession

172. The same rights apply to all despite of their country of origin and habitual residence. Therefore a foreigner has normally a similar right of inheritance as a Finnish citizen. However, if a Finnish citizen is not treated equally concerning the right to inherit than a citizen of that state, it is possible that a corresponding restriction regarding the citizens of the said state is issued by Decree (the Code of Inheritance, Chapter 1, section 3).

§3. The System of Descent

I. The Classes of Heirs

173. The statutory order of inheritance is based on the parentelic principle. Heirs are sorted into groups—called parentela—on the basis to which the relatives of a deceased have a right of inheritance. In each group there is a right of substitution and only if there are no heirs in a previous group, the right to inherit devolves on the next parentela. The right of substitution is unlimited in the first two groups. In the third group the substitution is restricted, though.

The first group of heirs who have the primary right to the estate includes the direct descendants (the deceased's children and their offspring). Each child receives an equal share of the inheritance. If a primary heir has died, his/her descendants take his/her place (this is called a right of substitution) and each branch receives an equal share (the Code of Inheritance, Chapter 2, section 1). Adopted children have the same inheritance rights as biological children and therefore no special rules concerning adoption and inheritance are provided in the Inheritance Code.[152]

174. The second group of heirs includes the secondary heirs who are the parents of the deceased. If each of the parents has died before the deceased, his/her share of the estate devolves on his or her offspring. Thus, the deceased's siblings and their offspring belong to the second parentela (the Code of Inheritance, Chapter 2, section 2.1). Also in this group of heirs each branch receives an equal share. If the deceased did not have or was not survived by any brothers or sisters or their children, but one of the parents of the deceased is still living, the parent receives the entire inheritance (the Code of Inheritance, Chapter 2, section 2.2). In case the deceased had stepbrothers or stepsisters, they receive—along with any full brothers or sisters—their share of what their father or mother would have received. If there are no full brothers or sisters or their descendants and if both parents have died, the whole of the estate devolves on the stepbrothers and stepsisters. If a stepbrother or stepsister has died, his or her descendants take his or her place.

The third group of heirs includes the grandparents of the deceased. In cases where the grandparents are not living, their share devolves on their children, i.e., the uncles and aunts of the deceased. In this group the right of substitution is limited as cousins do not have a right of inheritance (the Code of Inheritance, Chapter 2, section 2).

II. Forced Shares

175. The Code of Inheritance provides to heirs of the first parentela a primary right to a certain quota of the estate. In case of default, an heir can claim a forced share of the estate (in Finnish: *lakiosa*). A forced share consists of one half of the value of heir's portion of the inheritance according to the statutory parentelic system. For example, if the deceased was survived by two children, the statutory share of each is half, and the forced portion of each is one-fourth of the estate (the Code of Inheritance, Chapter 7, section 1).

176. In the calculation of the forced share, the value of whole of the estate is taken into account. In addition to this, value of certain lifetime transfers made by a deceased—e.g., an advancement—may be added to the computational estate. Also certain other gifts listed in the Code of Inheritance, Chapter 7, section 3, are added. An example of these is a gift given by a deceased during his/her lifetime in such circumstances that the gift is comparable with a bequest in a will. The same applies

152. Between 1925 and 1980 the adoption was based on the principle of weak adoption. In a weak adoption an adopted child has a right of inheritance from the biological parents (in a normal way) and from the adopting parents (with specific limitations concerning the rules of forced shares). The principle that the adoption is based on was changed by the Adoption Act 1980. According to its rules legal ties between the biological parents and the child are permanently terminated and a normal parent-child relationship created between the adoptive parent and the child. The principle of strong adoption is the basis of the regulation also in the new Adoption Law (22/2012, English translation can be found at: www.finlex.fi/fi/laki/kaannokset/2012/en20120022.pdf).

to a gift given by the deceased to his/her descendant or adopted child, or to their descendants, or a spouse of any of the same, if the purpose of the gift was to favor its recipient to the detriment of an heir entitled to a lawful share. In the above-mentioned cases the value of the conveyed property is—if the circumstances are not unusual—the same as to its value when a gift was transferred.

Also, disproportionate life insurance payments can be added to a computational estate in determining the forced shares of the estate. The requirement for this is that the deceased had designated a third party as the beneficiary. The added amount cannot exceed the amount of the policy (the Code of Inheritance, Chapter 7, section 4).

A deceased cannot infringe the right to a forced share by making a will, except in cases where there are lawful reasons for disinheritance and these are stipulated in a will. However, in determining the forced share, a person whom the deceased has disinherited in a will—or who for some other legal reason has no right to inherit—is taken into account in the calculations.

III. Claim for Support

177. Now, when lifespan is expected to be longer and longer, it is common that by the time inheritance is due, the children (the primary heirs) of the deceased are able to take care of their own maintenance. Still, there are provisions according to which certain persons can claim and receive support (in Finnish: *avustus*) from the estate. The support can be paid to a child of a deceased, his/her parents, his/her spouse or a person engaged to the deceased.

Also a surviving partner is entitled to claim for support, if he/she (a claimant) had lived in a common household with the deceased for at least five years. In case the common household has lasted for a shorter period of time, there is a possibility to claim also if the deceased and the claimant had a common child.[153]

178. The requirement for the payment is that it is needed for a reasonable livelihood or (in case of a child) upbringing and education. The payment can be sorted out in various ways; in the form of money, other property or as a usufruct. The starting point is that the support has priority over inheritances and bequests and is paid from the net estate (the Code of Inheritance, Chapter 8, sections 1–4). However, through the payment it is not possible to violate the widow's right to minimum protection (the Code of Inheritance, Chapter 3, section 1a).

In addition, pursuant to Chapter 8 of the Code of Inheritance an heir who had worked to assist the deceased in his/her business or profession, or in his/ her household can claim for compensation. The requirement is that the claimant has worked continuously without receiving reasonable compensation therefor and if there was no agreement between the deceased and the heir on compensation.

153. In this respect the cohabitation refers to partners to whom the Act on the Dissolution of the Household of Cohabiting Partners (26/2011) was applicable at the time of the death. *See also* Salla Silvola: National Report: Finland. Commission on European Family Law: Country Reports, 2015,,s. 25.

Compensation should be demanded within five years from the death of the deceased. However, if the work was performed more than ten years preceding the death of the deceased, the compensation is not payable as the claim is outdated.

In determining how much should be paid as a compensation, the Code of Inheritance, Chapter 8, section 5, lays down certain criteria that are taken into consideration; namely the assets of the estate, the type and amount of the work performed, the skill of the worker, the compensation received in kind or otherwise from the deceased and the other special circumstances. The compensation cannot infringe the right of an heir to a forced share or the rights of the widow under the Code of inheritance, Chapter 3, section 1a.

§4. The Legal Position of the Surviving Spouse

I. General

179. The parentelic principle is built on the kinship and accordingly, the surviving spouse is not included in any parentela. However, under certain circumstances—in case there are no lineal descendants—the estate devolves on the surviving spouse. Even in cases where a widow is not entitled to inherit the deceased spouse, he/she still has certain rights over the estate. The rights the widow is entitled to are partly based on matrimonial law as a marital right has to be realized to determine the computational value of the estate and the property that belongs to it. Partly the rights of a widow are based on inheritance law, including a right of support from the estate, a right of inheritance and a right to keep property of the estate in possession.

Hence, the widow's legal position is built on a combination of the matrimonial law and the inheritance law.

Interpretational starting point is to favor a surviving spouse. This means that in case of uncertainty as to how to interpret certain provision regarding widow's legal position, it should be interpreted and applied in such manner that the position of the widow is protected as far as possible.

II. The Influence of the Matrimonial Property

180. If a marriage is dissolved by the death of the spouse, the rules of the distribution of the matrimonial property are applied. According to the section 35 of the Marriage Act, the spouses have a marital right to each other's property in case where there are no reasons to treat property as separate (i.e., when no marriage settlement has been concluded). The marital right entitles both spouses—also the surviving spouse—to get one half of the net value of all of the spouse's property subject to the marital right. In case the deceased spouse's net property exceeds the surviving spouse's property in terms of value, the widow is entitled to compensation payment under the generally applicable rules. Therefore, the marital regime has to be dissolved to define the distributable estate.

181. In certain respects the death changes the rules of the distribution in favor of the widow. If the net property of a widow exceeds to that of the deceased (if he/she has been the wealthier party in the marriage), he/she does not have to pay compensation to the heirs of a deceased spouse (the Marriage Act, section 103.2). In legal literature this is called "the distribution privilege" (in Finnish: *tasinkoprivilegi*). According to a case law, thus, the right against the heirs is interpreted to protect the widow personally and is not applicable if the surviving spouse dies before the division of matrimonial regime has ended.[154] Narrow interpretation of the rule has, however, been contested in legal literature.

In cases where the marriage ceases to the death of either spouse, the estate property is administered between the surviving spouse and the heirs of the deceased spouse. The heirs have to act unanimously (so-called consensus principle) and, for instance, decide together what property they will hand over in the distribution of matrimonial property. Instead of property, the heirs may hand over money to the value determined for the property at the time of the distribution.[155] Both the heirs and a spouse have a right to claim for adjustment of the distribution.

III. A Right of Inheritance

182. In case the deceased was not survived by any primary heirs (heirs from the first group), but was married at the time of his/her death, the widow has a right of inheritance (Code of Inheritance, Chapter 3, section 1). There is an exception to the rule, though, since a spouse loses the right of inheritance if the divorce proceedings were pending at the time of death, unless there can be proven to exist special circumstances.[156]

183. If the surviving spouse inherits the deceased spouse, the distribution of matrimonial property is not necessary since all property of the deceased devolves on the widow. The inherited property does not devolve on the widow and his/her heirs absolutely, since the secondary heirs of the deceased (heirs from the second parentela) have a right to the inheritance but they have to wait until the surviving spouse dies. After this the estate is divided between the secondary heirs and widow's own heirs in equal shares (the Code of Inheritance, Chapter 3, section 1.2). The situation is computationally somewhat different though if, at the death of the first deceased spouse, all of the spouses' property was not subject to the marital right and instead, one or both spouses had separate property. In these cases the property of the first deceased spouse constitutes a corresponding share of the estate of the surviving spouse at the death of the latter (the Code of Inheritance, Chapter 3, section 2).

154. *See* Eva Gottberg: Study on the Matrimonial Property Regimes and the Property of Unmarried Couples in Private International Law and Internal Law. National Report: Finland. Commission Européenne JAI/A3/2001/03, p. 19 and for case law, i.e., the Supreme Court case KKO 2001:12.

155. Note s. 103a of the Marriage Act according to which the widow may take from property (not excluded from the marital right) the necessary household goods and tools and other movables he or she needs in order to carry on his or her business.

156. The Code of Inheritance, Ch. 3, s. 7. The burden of proof lies on the widow to show that the special circumstances existed at the time of death, *see* the Supreme Court case KKO 2016:60.

Even though there are secondary heirs, the legal position of a spouse in respect to inherited property is strong. He/she receives an unrestricted right to dispose of property. The surviving spouse may sell the property or give it as a gift. Secondary heirs are not protected against these dispositions during the lifetime of a surviving spouse.[157]

184. However, the widow's right of inheritance covers only *inter vivos* transactions. The surviving spouse cannot make any testamentary disposition that would have an effect on the secondary heirs rights (the Code of Inheritance, Chapter 3, section 1.2). If the surviving spouse infringes the rights of secondary heirs in this respect, the disposition is not valid against them.

The inheritance right of a surviving spouse is not protected against the will of the deceased spouse since he/she has not a right to a forced share. The surviving spouse is legally protected by using another means. He/she has a right to keep the estate or part of it in his/her possession despite the rights of primary heirs to a forced share or beneficiaries under a will.

IV. The Right to Keep the Estate Undivided

185. In case the surviving spouse has no right of inheritance due to the rights of primary heirs or the beneficiaries under a will, he/she still has a right to keep the estate undivided; in other words, in his/her possession (the Code of Inheritance, Chapter 3, section 1a.1). At the first stage, a widow may possess all of the property but if the heir demands the estate distribution, the protection of the surviving spouse diminishes to cover the common home of spouses and household movables. This is called the minimum protection of the surviving spouse (in Finnish: *lesken vähimmäissuoja*). The benefit lasts the lifetime of a widow and in practice it can be deemed to be very important from the perspective of social protection of a surviving spouse.[158]

The protection cannot be affected or removed by a will or a marriage settlement. The right of possession (the minimum protection) is ensured even if it infringes the primary heir's right to a forced share. Even though the ownership of the property may devolve on the heir as an inheritance, the rights of the heir are burdened by the widow's benefit of possession.

186. It is possible, though, that the surviving spouse's right to a minimum protection is hindered, but only if he/she owns a similar dwelling compared to spouses'

157. It is possible for secondary heirs to claim for compensation (after the widow's death) if the property of the surviving spouse has significantly decreased in value, due to transactions made by the widow. If the surviving spouse has donated the property and the donee knew (or should have known) that the conveyance infringed the secondary heirs rights, it is possible that the donee has to return either the gift or its value (the Inheritance Code, Ch. 3, s. 3.) Another exception to the equal division follows if the property has increased in value and the widow has received the (corresponding) property as an inheritance, a bequest or a gift. In addition, if the increase in the value is due to the gainful employment or business of the surviving spouse after the death of the first deceased spouse, this benefits the heirs of the surviving spouse (the Inheritance Code, Ch. 3, s. 4).
158. Kirsti Kurki-Suonio: National Report: Property Relationships Between Spouses – Finland. Commission on European Family Law: Country Reports, 2008, p. 26.

common home. The protection cannot be rejected claiming that the widow owns an apartment that would be suitable for his/her home if it is not similar enough in terms of size, location and quality to the common dwelling of the spouses (this interpretation was confirmed in a Supreme Court case KKO 1992:94).

A surviving spouse may lose the right to keep the estate undivided if divorce proceedings were pending when the spouse died (the Code of Inheritance, Chapter 3, section 7). There is an exception to the rule if the surviving spouse is able to prove special circumstances in order to activate his/her rights of possession - for instance, that the spouses have reached an agreement during the consideration period that they will not obtain a final divorce (for an interpretation of special circumstances *see* a Supreme Court case KKO 2016:60).

V. Support from the Estate

187. A widow may claim support from the estate if it can be established that it is necessary for his/her livelihood. Support can be paid from the net estate in any form (money, property, usufruct etc.) but only if it can be deemed reasonable. Therefore, a right for support is not an automatic right. In considering whether a support should be paid or not, one has to take into account what rights the surviving spouse is entitled to under Chapters 3 and 25 of the Inheritance Code (the Code of Inheritance, Chapter 8, section 2). Each case is decided depending on the individual financial circumstances of a surviving spouse.

If a will infringes widow's right to support, a primary right is that of a widow and will is not valid inasmuch this is necessary to pay support to the surviving spouse. In the absence of persuasive reasons to the contrary, the payment of support cannot infringe on the right of an heir to a forced share.

§5. The Rights of the State

188. The inheritance devolves on the State if the deceased was not survived by even a single heir belonging to one of the groups of parentela, did not leave a surviving spouse or a beneficiary under a will (the Code of Inheritance, Chapter 5). In these cases, the State Treasure Office (in Finnish: *Valtiokonttori*) is responsible for the administration of the estate.

In all cases the State will not keep the inheritance property. Instead, the property can be conveyed to—the estate in whole or in part—a person close to the deceased. In this respect, kinship is not set as a requirement and property can be conveyed to for instance a cohabitee of a deceased. The conveyance can be made if it is deemed reasonable in light of the circumstances (the Code of Inheritance, Chapter 5, section 2).[159] The property may also be transferred to the municipality where the deceased was last living. In case the deceased owned immovable property, it can also be conveyed to the municipality of its location.

159. If the inventory value of the estate exceeds EUR 750,000, the decision of the transfer is made by the Council of State.

In some cases there are deemed to exist special reasons for keeping the property for the State. However, this does not have to prevent the property being given to a person close to the deceased, if it is deemed that the transfer would correspond to the last will of the deceased (the Code of Inheritance, Chapter 5, section 2).

According to statistics, every year the State Treasury is notified of approximately 600 persons who have died without heirs, representing around 1% of all deceased people. About 60% of the people who have died without heirs had drawn up a will.[160]

160. *See* the webpages of the State Treasury, at: http://www.statetreasury.fi/en-US/Citizens_and_Communities/Inheritance_of_people_who_have_died_without_heirs.

Chapter 3. Testamentary Succession

189. The estate devolves in whole according to the provisions of the Code of Inheritance if the deceased did not dispose of his/her property by a will (in Finnish: *testamentti*). A will is the most important tool in the estate planning and it is quite common to draw a will in Finland. Under the provisions of the Code of Inheritance the deceased has a right to self-determination, meaning that the testator has wide discretion as regards content of his/her will. There are, however, certain substantive limits as testator cannot include to his/her will dispositions that are for instance against good morals.

By a will the statutory order of inheritance can be overridden. If the will infringes the right to a forced share, it does not make the will invalid but it might be that the forced share prevents the fulfillment of the testamentary bequest in full or partly. However, if the deceased was not survived by an heir from a first parentela (primary heir), he/she is able to bequeath all of his/her property to the person or persons he/she chooses. If the testator was married, though, the minimum protection of a widow cannot be overridden by a will and consequently the benefits (a right of possession to a certain estate property) that the widow enjoys have an effect on the rights of the beneficiaries under a will.

§1. The Capacity to Make a Will

190. Under the provisions of the Code of Inheritance, a person who has reached the age of 18 years may dispose of his/her property by a will (the Code of Inheritance, Chapter 9, section 1). There are exceptions to this rule, though. If a person concludes marriage prior to reaching the age of 18 years, he/she obtains testamentary capacity. One cannot lose testamentary capacity acquired through a marriage if the marriage is later dissolved before reaching majority. Also a minor who has reached the age of fifteen is independently able to draw a will with regard to property he/she is entitled to administer. This property includes minor's own earnings from work, proceeds from these earnings and property purchased with them (the Code of Inheritance, Chapter 9, section 1). It is worth stressing in this respect that every testator has to understand the meaning of a will and legal implications drawing it up in order the will to gain validity.

I. Form

191. The form of the will is regulated in detail in the provisions of the Inheritance Code. In judicial practice the form is interpreted rigorously. Consequently, if the legal requirements are not followed, the will is not to have legal effects.

A will must be made in writing but it does not have to be typed. It has to be signed by the testator and witnessed by two witnesses (the Code of Inheritance, Chapter 10, section 1). The witnesses must be simultaneously present when the testator signs the will or acknowledges his/her earlier signature to them. The testator does not have to unveil the substance of the will to the witnesses. However, they have to understand that the document in question—and what they witness with their signatures—is a last will of the deceased.

192. It is possible for the witnesses to certify their attestation and to note in a will any other factors that they consider relevant with regard to its validity. This so-called certification (in Finnish: *todistuslauselma*) is not obligatory but if it is included in a will, it is considered that the requirements for the attestation are followed. Therefore, if a claim is brought to the court based on the faults in witnessing the will, the burden of proof lies on the party raising the claim (the Inheritance Code, Chapter 10, section 2).[161]

There is a provision in the Inheritance Code that determines who is able to act as a witness of a will. A person under 15 years of age or who suffers of a mental defect, is not able to act as a witness. Witnesses cannot be close to a testator as the Inheritance Code states: "a testament cannot be attested by the spouse or a direct ascendant or descendant or in-law of the testator, nor by the testator's brother or sister or the spouse of such, nor by the testator's adoptive parents or adopted children" (the Code of Inheritance, Chapter 10, section 4). A witness must be uninterested and cannot benefit under the will. Therefore "no one shall attest a disposition which benefits himself or herself or his or her spouse or a person who is related to him or her" (the Code of Inheritance, Chapter 10, section 4). However, it has been specifically stated in the Inheritance Code that even if a person is appointed to act as an executor of a will, he/she is still able to witness it—even though he/she receives reasonable remuneration for the work done as an executor.

193. If a person is not able to follow the standard form in making a will, for instance in cases of serious illness or other compelling reason, it is possible to make an oral will (emergency will). Thus, in order it to gain legal validity it is required that there are two witnesses simultaneously present (the Code of Inheritance, Chapter 10, section 3). Under exceptional circumstances it is even possible to make a will without witnesses by way of a personally hand-written and signed document (holographic will). The requirements for making a valid emergency or holographic will are the same: there have to be compelling reasons for not following the standard form of a will. The obstacle may be either physical or mental. An example of a case where a holographic will may be deemed valid is suicide. An emergency or a holographic will lapses to be valid if the testator has for three months (after the obstacle has ceased to exist) had the opportunity make a will following the standard form.

194. In Finland there are no register of wills administered by public authorities. The testator may choose where to keep his/her will. It can be kept in a bank deposit box or at home, sometimes a copy is given to a lawyer who has helped to draw it up.[162]

161. The rule of was confirmed in a Supreme Court case KKO 2016:40 where it was held that even though the witnesses (who had certified their attestation) did not remember the event of their attestation, the burden of proof was still on the party who contested the validity of a will and brought the claim to the court.

162. *See* the European Network of Registers of Wills Association and an information sheet explaining how to register and to find a will in Finland at: www.arert.eu/Finland.html.

§2. Different Types of Wills

195. A disposition of a will can be either universal bequest (in Finnish: *yleistestamentti*) or a legacy (in Finnish: *erityisjälkisäädös, legaatti*). It is important to separate these wills in relation to the benefit in question, since this has legal effects as regards the rights and status of the beneficiary in the estate administration.

If a will provides that a beneficiary inherits the whole estate, a fraction of it (i.e., one-third) or all that is left after executing the other provisions under a will, the bequest is defined as universal by nature. A person holding a status of a universal beneficiary has a right in respect to estate property that is similar to that of a statutory heir. Consequently, a universal beneficiary is one of the shareholders in the deceased's estate (the Code of Inheritance, Chapter 18, section 1), even if the will has been contested (the Code of Inheritance, Chapter 18, section 2).

196. Instead of giving such a general right to a beneficiary, a testator may use a legacy. A testamentary disposition that gives the beneficiary title to a specific object or rights to property inferior to ownership (rights of use and/or rights to the proceeds from specific property) are defined as a legacy. A legacy beneficiary does not take part to the administration of the estate. The legacy is fulfilled from an undistributed estate as soon as it is possible (the Code of Inheritance, Chapter 22, section 1).

The extent of the rights under a will may vary in other ways, as well, and in this respect one can classify different types of wills. First, a testator may choose to confer an ownership to a beneficiary in a will. In other words, a will gives a beneficiary a title to all of the estate's property, to a fraction of all the property or to a specific property. Accordingly, a beneficiary is free to make transactions inter vivos and mortis causa in respect to the property received from a testator (in Finnish: *omistusoikeustestamentti*).

197. A testator may also choose to give limited ownership to the beneficiary. It means that a beneficiary acquires a full ownership to testator's property. He/she holds owner's status except for transactions mortis causa. The reason for the restriction is that the original will includes a disposition according to which there is a second beneficiary or beneficiaries in respect to the inherited property. Therefore at beneficiary's death the property is distributed to the secondary heirs in accordance with the (original) will (in Finnish: *rajoitettu omistusoikeustestamentti*).It is also possible to give a beneficiary a right to possess and use the property, whereas the ownership is given to some other person (in Finnish: *käyttöoikeustestamentti*).[163] A beneficiary who enjoys the right of use, is able to possess the property and the person holding the owner's status cannot intervene. However, if the person using a property mismanages the property and this obviously compromises owner's interests, it is possible that a court appoints a person for its administration (the Code of Inheritance, Chapter 12, section 9). A person holding a right of use is not able to sell or donate the property or make

163. Right of use under a will is regulated in detail in Ch. 12 of the Inheritance Code. These provisions are applicable, though, only if not otherwise stated in the will. Note that it is not obligatory that there is an owner as long as the beneficiary holds a right of use. It is therefore possible that the ownership is conferred at the time the right of use ceases to exist at the death of its holder (in Finnish: *omistajattoman tilan testamentti*).

mortis causa dispositions in respect of the property.[164] It is not permissible to transfer the right of use under a will (the Code of Inheritance, Chapter 12, section 4). Wills granting rights of usufruct are quite common in estate planning in Finland[165] and often made in the form of joint wills (in Finnish: *keskinäinen testamentti*).

198. A will can also grant a beneficiary an inferior right than the right of use of the property. A testator may choose to give a person a right to the proceeds from the property (in Finnish: *tuotto-oikeustestamentti*). Right to the proceeds does not give a right to use the property. A beneficiary's right is protected as a beneficiary holding the ownership of the property cannot reduce the right to proceeds; the right is secured even in cases where the owner conveys the property to a third person.

§3. Joint Will

199. Reciprocal bequests are permissible and can be made between spouses, cohabitees and any other persons in favor of each other. A joint will is therefore valid. Usually it is drawn up as being conditional on both sides and therefore the validity of one testamentary disposition is dependent on whether the other gains effect.

Thus, even though a joint will is a combination of two wills, it is not construed or defined in terms of a contract. An agreement pertaining to the estate of a living person is invalid (the Inheritance Code, Chapter 17, section 1). Therefore, the general rules of making, revoking, interpreting and executing a will are applied to joint wills, as well.

§4. Revocation of a Will

200. A testator is entitled to change his/her mind at any time. Also revocation of a will is always and under any circumstances possible as nobody is able to make a binding promise or contract not to revoke a will (the Code of Inheritance, Chapter 10, section 5). If a will is revoked and not replaced by a new one, the statutory order of inheritance is applicable.

164. The holder of the right of use cannot transfer (or i.e., pledge) the property subject to the right without the specific permission of the owner. Under exceptional circumstances, though, movable property can be conveyed if its renewal is deemed necessary or if the property is art of an industrial or some other enterprise and the transfer belongs in the sphere of sensible management (the Inheritance Code, Ch. 12, s. 4). Also a court may grant a permission for a transfer movable property—but not if it can be shown that the property is of special value to the person owning it.

165. Estate tax planning is one of the reasons why a disposition granting a usufruct is quite popular choice in estate planning as one does not have to pay inheritance tax on the right of usufruct. In addition, the right of use decreases the value according to which the tax of the owners is calculated, based on the values shown in the estate inventory deed. Therefore, a will granting a right of use is often considered a good method to minimize inheritance tax. *See* more closely the webpages of Tax Administration at: www.vero.fi/en/individuals/property/inheritance/how_to_value_the_estate_of_someone_who_/.

The revocation of a will is free in form. A testator may destroy a will for instance by tearing it up. A will may also be amended at any time prior to the deceased's death. A standard form has to be followed in making an amendment to the will since this is deemed as drawing up a new will.

Joint wills are defined as a combination of two or more separate wills, and therefore also they are revocable in respect to each of the testators. However, a unilateral revocation of reciprocal dispositions of a will may lead to losing rights under another will (the Code of Inheritance, Chapter 10, section 7).

§5. Restrictions

I. Forced Share to the Estate

201. The testator's freedom to include provisions to his/her will may in some cases be de facto restricted. If the will infringes rights of heirs of the first parentela to a forced share, their right is protected (the Code of Inheritance, Chapter 7, section 1). It is noteworthy, though, that a forced share is not compulsory share that is paid from the estate automatically. In all cases it is up to the protected heir whether he/she explicitly claims that he or she wants a forced share be paid from the estate. The claim must be made to the beneficiary under a will within six months of the heir having being informed of the deceased's death and of the infringement of the heir's right to a forced share (due to the deceased having left a will, the Code of Inheritance, Chapter 7, section 5). The claim have to be made in verifiable manner, for instance by means of a process server.

The forced share amounts to one half of the value of the statutory share that according to the provisions of the Inheritance Code would otherwise devolve on the heir (the Code of Inheritance, Chapter 7, section 1). In determining the value of a forced share, also those persons whom the deceased has disinherited in a will or who for some other reason are not eligible to inherit the deceased, are taken into account in calculations (the Code of Inheritance, Chapter 7, section 2). Also lifetime gifts made by the testator can be taken into consideration in determining the computational estate in this respect (the Code of Inheritance, Chapter 7, section 3).

202. To the extent that a will infringes the right of an heir to a forced portion and he/she has claimed for it, the will is invalid only in relation to such an heir. This might prevent the execution of a specific disposition. However, a beneficiary of a will has a right to pay a computational value of a forced share in money if it has not been specifically forbidden in a will. In other words, the claim can be considered as an obligation. The payment has to take place within a reasonable period of time specified by the heir (the Code of Inheritance, Chapter 7, section 5).

§6. Distribution of a Farm

203. The Code of Inheritance in its original form did not include any special rules concerning distribution of a farm,[166] but the law was changed in 1983. Application of special rules (the Inheritance Code, Chapter 25) has since been possible in respect to property that serves an agricultural operation. The purpose of the ruling is to promote the transfer of a farm in an undivided and viable form to an heir in the estate distribution. The provisions are applicable, however, only if the testator has not made other dispositions in a will. A testator is, thus, free to hinder the applicability of these rules. In case a testator has not included any such dispositions in his/her will, also the shareholders in the estate may agree not to apply the special regulation concerning distribution of agricultural property. Provisions are not obligatory by nature.

For the purposes of the provisions, the viable farm is defined as a farm that suffices as the main livelihood of the farmer and his/her family. Moreover, a suitable agricultural successor is defined as an heir or a universal beneficiary under a will who has this status at the time of distribution and who has the necessary professional competence to pursue an agricultural business. A suitable agricultural successor has the right to demand that a viable farm is allotted undivided, and with any agricultural movables, into his/her share of the estate.[167] The suitable agricultural successor is obligated to farm the property for at least ten years' time.

In the distribution of matrimonial property of the spouses, if carried out after the death of the other spouse, a surviving spouse is able to demand that a farm should be allocated to his/her share. Again, the requirement for accepting the widow's claim is that he/she has necessary professional competence to pursue an agricultural business (the Code of Inheritance, Chapter 25, section 9).[168]

§7. Interpretation of a Will

204. If uncertainty of the meaning of a will or its individual disposition is raised, the Inheritance Code, Chapter 11, section 1, guides the interpretation. It reads:

166. *See* Heikki E. S. Mattila: Les successions agricoles et la structure de la société. Un étude en droit comparé. Helsinki 1979.
167. In case competing claims are raised, the Inheritance Code includes provisions on how to decide who is given preference. It should be given to a person who has the best professional competence to pursue farming. However, an heir who has clearly better chances to work elsewhere is not given a preference over a person who does not have earning potential off the farm. Another factor that has to be taken into consideration is whether an heir (suitable agricultural successor) lives permanently on a farm and has participated actively in the farming. Such an heir has a preference over the others. If after taking all above-mentioned factors into consideration and the successor cannot be chosen, the choice is made by drawing lots (the Code of Inheritance, Ch. 25, s. 3).
168. The Inheritance Code include detailed provisions on how to value a farm in a distribution and how to ensure a heir's right to a forced share when Ch. 25 is applicable and property is allotted to preferred heir's share in the distribution. *See* i.e., Inheritance Code, Ch. 25, s. 2.

> A testament shall be construed in accordance with what can be deemed to be the will of the testator. If the testament, due to a typographical error or an erroneous expression, has received a content other than what the testator had intended, the testament shall nevertheless be executed if the true intent can be discovered.

The interpretation leans primarily on the text of a will: what is included in it—in its linguistic form—and what can be construed to be the correct meaning when it is interpreted as a whole. The purpose of the interpretation is to ascertain the true intention of the testator and in its determination one has to ascribe to the words of the will. In cases of uncertainty, the will is construed as a whole and available extrinsic material is taken into account if necessary.

205. Subjective interpretation is possible, thus, to a certain respect. If a will is contested and it is claimed that the text of the will and the testator's intent are in conflict, the burden of proof lies on the party making such claims. The threshold of a burden of proof is set quite high in such cases—especially if the claimed interpretation of testator's wishes has no actual connection to the linguistic formulation of a will. If it can be proven that the will, due to a typographical error or an erroneous expression, was written in a different way than what the testator intended, the will can be interpreted following the true intent if it can be discovered (the Code of Inheritance, Chapter 11, section 1).

There is a special rule for cases where the testator's fiancé or a spouse has been designated as a beneficiary and the engagement is broken or the marriage dissolved thereafter for reasons other than the death of the testator. The same applies in respect of a will according to which a spouse is a beneficiary and a divorce was pending in a court at the time of death of the testator. The default interpretation is that the disposition of the will is invalid if it cannot be proven that the testator wanted otherwise. Therefore the interpretation depends on the circumstances of each individual case (the Code of Inheritance, Chapter 11, section 8).

If a beneficiary dies before his/her right under the will comes into force, the descendants of the beneficiary are entitled to take his/her place if they would have had the right to inherit the testator (the Code of Inheritance, Chapter 11, section 6).

Chapter 4. Dispositions Inter Vivos Related to the Estate

206. Transactions among living (inter vivos) are in practice an important part of one's estate planning. Naturally, a person can transfer and convey his/her property inter vivos according to provisions of property law. However, the Inheritance Code aims at ensuring the equality of division of the estate between the heirs. If a deceased has—during his/her lifetime—given to a descent (or to some other person close to him/her) benefits, gifts etc. that are atypically large in value, these will be taken into account when calculating computational shares on estate distribution. Consequently, even though a person enjoys lifelong freedom to dispose of his/her property as he/she wishes, inter vivos transfers are taken into account in the distribution under certain circumstances: these circumstances are stipulated in detail in the provisions of the Inheritance Code.

There are legal restrictions as to what transactions a person can do, thus, since inheritance contracts (contracts pertaining to the estate of a person still living) are invalid (the Inheritance Code, Chapter 17, section 1). In other words, if the validity of a certain transfer or other legal act is connected to a death of a party, such transactions have to be made in a form of a will.

§1. Donations and Gifts

207. According to a so-called hotchpot provision of the Inheritance Code beneficiaries have to bring into account donations and gifts that was conveyed to them from the deceased and prior to his/her death.[169] In each case it must be determined, though, whether the gift under the circumstances should be defined as advancement (in Finnish: *ennakkoperintö*) or not. If the value of the gift is not disproportionate to the circumstances of the donor, it is not taken into account in the distribution (the Inheritance Code, Chapter 6, section 4). In this respect it should be stressed that all benefits with a value can be defined as advancement and should be taken into account in the distribution. An example is a right of use to a flat, etc.

208. The expenses incurred by the parents by supporting, raising and educating a child should not be deducted from the inheritance of the said child. However, if supporting and/or educating the child has incurred atypical and extraordinary expenses, these expenses may be considered as advancement partly or in full in the estate distribution (the Inheritance Code, Chapter 6, section 2). In defining whether these expenses are extraordinary, one has to take account the individual, financial circumstances of each family.

209. The provisions of the Inheritance Code are based on a presumption that the deceased has wanted the estate to be distributed evenly among the heirs even though he/she has given gifts to some of them prior to his/her death and therefore the heir who has received advancements inherits a smaller computational share of the estate. The Inheritance Code, Chapter 6, section 1, provides the following:

169. For taxation of the donations *see* the webpages of Tax Administration at: www.vero.fi/en-US/Individuals/Inheritance/Gifts_given_before_death(15354).

Unless otherwise stipulated or unless a contrary intention can be inferred from the circumstances, what the decedent during his or her lifetime gave to a direct descendant shall be considered as an advancement and deducted from the inheritance of the latter. If the recipient of the advancement is an heir who is not a direct descendant, the said deduction shall be made only if, at the time the property was given, it was so stipulated or such an intention is to be inferred from the circumstances.

210. Consequently, the deceased's right to self-determination covers also advancements to a certain respect. He/she may stipulate whether a gift given by him/her should be taken into account in the distribution. However, the freedom is not limitless since equality among direct descendants is protected in cases where estate planning includes dispositions inter vivos. Even though a deceased has stipulated that the gift should not be considered as advancement, it is still possible under the Inheritance Code, Chapter 7, section 3, that a gift is equated with the will (in Finnish: *testamenttiin rinnastuva lahja*) and therefore should be deducted from the inheritance of its recipient. It is also possible to do the same if the lifetime gift given to a direct descent or its descent or a spouse and the main purpose of the transfer was to favor the recipient to the detriment of an heir entitled to a forced portion (in Finnish: *suosiolahja*).

211. In determining the computational effects of the gift in the distribution, the value of the gift is considered to be the value that it had when received (the Inheritance Code, Chapter 6, section 5). Date of the valuation may also change due to special circumstances. An example is a case where a deceased has given same kind of property (i.e., a flat) to his/her children during a longer period of time, for instance within twenty years of time. In such a case an equal treatment may require that the date of valuation is the same in respect to all of the donations. Again here, the testator is able to stipulate otherwise and he/she has a freedom to define the computational value of the conveyance. In addition, if the deceased received remuneration for the gift, the remuneration should be deducted from the value of the gift in the distribution.

If the entire value of advancement cannot be deducted from the inheritance devolving on an heir, he/she does not have to return the balance to the estate. However, the deceased may stipulate otherwise when handing out the advancement (the Inheritance Code, Chapter 6, section 6). If there is not enough property in the estate to pay forced shares, an action for its supplement can be brought to the court (the Inheritance Code, Chapter 7, sections 8–10).

It should be noted that gifts between spouses are valid without taking any special measures and also in relation to the heirs of the deceased spouse.

§2. Donatio Mortis Causa

212. The donatio mortis causa is a gift made in contemplation of a death of a donor and not accepted in the Finnish legal system. This is confirmed in the Inheritance Code, Chapter 17, section 2, according to which if a gift is not fulfilled during the donor's lifetime, it may gain legal effects at the death of the donor only if provisions concerning wills have been followed and the gift has been made in the form of a will.

§3. Trusts

213. Trust-institution is not known in Finnish legal system. Therefore, the creation of trust is not possible.[170]

§4. Insurance Contracts

214. It is quite common that a person concludes insurance contracts that relate to his/her person, such as a life insurance.[171] Life insurances have certain legal effects in the estate distribution, as well, as regulated in the Inheritance Code, Chapter 7, section 4. It provides that if the deceased has taken out life insurance and a third party is designated as the beneficiary,[172] the premiums paid by the deceased should be added to the assets of the estate in its distribution. The requirement for it is that the premiums have been atypical in value and therefore disproportionate in relation to the circumstances and assets of the estate. The maximum addition cannot exceed the amount of the policy. In addition, if the deceased has received remuneration for the designation of the assignment of the policy, the consideration that the deceased has received is deducted from the premiums in the distribution.[173]

170. On the assessment of the legal effects of foreign trusts from the perspective of Finnish legal system *see* , e.g., Tuulikki Mikkola: Enforcement of Foreign Trusts in Finland. The European Legal Forum, 1/2011, p. 33.

171. For statistics *see* the webpages of Finance Finland at: www.finanssiala.fi/en/materials/presentations/Pages/default.aspx and Official Statistics of Finland: Insurance Activities (e-publication). *See also* Insurance portfolios and payments of non-life insurance companies 2015. Statistics Finland, at: www.stat.fi/til/vato/2015/vato_2015_2016-11-21_tau_006_en.html.

172. It is common to designate "next of kin" as a beneficiary of the insurance contract. The meaning and interpretation of the designation may be dependent on the circumstances of the case. In a Supreme Court case KKO 2004:40 it was decided that the term "next of kin" referred to a cohabitee, since the cohabitee was also an only beneficiary under a will.

173. For the taxation of life insurances *see* the webpages of Tax Administration at: www.vero.fi/en/detailed-guidance/guidance/47830/guidance_on_tax_on_insurance_premium2/.

Chapter 5. Acquisition, Administration, and Distribution of the Estate

§1. General

215. Inheritance is defined as a process during which the property of the deceased is firstly administered and secondly transferred to the beneficiaries. Only after the estate has been completely wound up and administered—the obligations of the deceased fulfilled and the rights of legatees asserted—can the net property be transferred to the legal heirs and universal beneficiaries under a will. Thus, there is no maximum time during which the estate has to be wound up and the estate distributed. It can even be left undistributed as contracted by the heirs.

The debts of the deceased person are paid from the estate's assets and beneficiaries are not personally responsible for them. There is an exception to this rule; if a beneficiary, who is responsible for drawing up the estate inventory, has neglected the obligation and the inventory is not submitted by the deadline, a beneficiary can be held to be personally liable for the deceased's debts (the Inheritance Code, Chapter 21, sections 1–2).

The beneficiaries will also be liable for obligations contracted by them on behalf of the estate (the Inheritance Code, Chapter 21, section 4).

§2. The Seisin

216. It is mandatory to administer and settle the estate before it is distributed. However, the way in which it is done is voluntary. There are three different options. The first one (and the default system) is a private administration of an estate (regulated in Chapter 18 of the Code of Inheritance). It starts at the time of the deceased's death. Those who can take part in the administration, called shareholders of the estate, parties to the estate (in Finnish: *kuolinpesän osakkaat*), are named and specified in the Code of Inheritance. They include the legal heirs and the universal beneficiaries under a will. A legacy beneficiary under a will does not take part to the administration of the estate.

217. The surviving spouse is a shareholder until the distribution of matrimonial property has been carried out. However, in case the widow does not have a marital right to the property of the other spouse, he/she cannot take part in the administration as a shareholder unless he/she is an heir or a universal beneficiary. It is also stipulated in the Inheritance Code, Chapter 18, section 1, that a person who has the right to inherit or receive under a will after the death of another, primary heir or universal beneficiary, is a shareholder in the estate of this latter person, but not in the estate of the first deceased.

218. It is therefore possible for the deceased to use a will as a tool by which he/she can affect to the administration of the estate. For instance, by conclusion of a marriage settlement excluding the marital right of the spouses or by drawing a will including a disposition of a legacy, a deceased may mould the way the estate is being administered and by whom.

219. 208 The second possible form of administration is an official one. Upon an application the court has to appoint an administrator to the estate. If the petition for the official administrator is made, the court has no discretion whether to appoint an administrator or not. Any of the shareholders can decide to file a petition and no reasons are needed thereto. A court order may also be issued on the petition of a person who has been appointed as an executor in a will (the Inheritance Code, Chapter 19, section 1).

An application may also be submitted by a legatee under a will or a person to whom an heir or a universal beneficiary under the testament has transferred his or her share in the estate. Thus, in these cases the application must state reasons why an official administration is necessary in order to ensure the fulfillment of the bequest. The application may also be filed by a person entitled to claim for support from the estate. The applicant does not have to be a shareholder but the requirement for accepting the petition is, thus, that it is deemed necessary in order to enforce the claim (the Inheritance Code, Chapter 19, section 1). In addition, a creditor of a deceased is able to apply for an administrator (the Inheritance Code, Chapter 19, section 2).

220. Once an estate is transferred to an estate distributor, the shareholders' joint management ceases; the administrator is obliged to wind up the estate without delay and undertake any measures necessary thereto (the Inheritance Code, Chapter 19, section 12). The administrator represents the estate in relation to third parties (the Inheritance Code, Chapter 19, section 13) and can be sued in matters concerning the estate.

221. The Inheritance Code, Chapter 19, section 4, reads that the court should appoint as an estate administrator a person who can be presumed capable of settling the estate with the skill demanded by the type of the estate and who accepts the appointment. It follows that even a shareholder may be appointed for the task of an estate administrator (in case there is consensus among other shareholders) whereas a shareholder can never be appointed to act as an estate distributor.

A deceased may also affect how his/her estate is administered as the deceased may nominate a person to act as an executor of a will (the Code of Inheritance, Chapter 19, section 21). Even though an executor is appointed in a will, it is possible to petition for an appointment of an administrator but an executor has a right to be nominated as an administrator unless there exist certain special reasons why this should not happen (the Inheritance Code, Chapter 19, section 4).

222. The shareholders may also agree that it is in their common interest to manage the estate jointly and to leave it undistributed until further notice or for a specified period of time. This is called an agreement on joint administration. It cannot be concluded if the estate is in an official administration, meaning that a court has already appointed an estate administrator, or if an executor is nominated in a will and the executor has no competency to accept such an agreement according to the dispositions included in the will (the Inheritance Code, Chapter 24, section 1). The agreement on joint administration binds and a shareholder cannot apply the court to nominate an administrator after its conclusion, as long as the agreement is in effect.

§3. The Administration of the Estate

223. In private administration the shareholders of the estate must follow a consensus principle, not the majority principle. They have to undertake all measures and make even minor decisions concerning administration jointly and unanimously. The shareholders are together the representatives of the estate in respect of third parties and they can both sue and be sued in matters that concern winding up the estate. Only an action that is deemed urgent can be undertaken by one of the shareholders (or a minority of shareholders) even if the consent of all the shareholders cannot be obtained (the Code of Inheritance, Chapter 18, section 1).

In official administration the estate administrator is obliged to take any action necessary to wind up the estate. The administrator manages day-to-day business and practical matters related to the estate property. Thus, the assets of the estate cannot be mixed with property belonging to the administrator or to some other person. The monetary assets of the estate have to be deposited in the name of the estate (the Inheritance Code, Chapter 19, section 15).

224. The estate administrator represents the estate in respect of third parties and can sue and be sued in matters concerning the estate (the Code of Inheritance, Chapter 19, section 13). As a rule, the shareholders are excluded from the decision-making. Although the administrator has to consult beneficiaries before obtaining certain measures (considered important to the beneficiaries), the administrator may act even without their unanimous consent.[174]

The purpose of the administration is to settle the estate in such a way that the estate property can be distributed without detriment to anyone whose right is dependent on the winding up of the estate. One of the primary purposes of the administration is paying off the debts. If it is noted that the estate is indebted, the estate administrator tries to reach an agreement with the creditors to their satisfaction. If the agreement is not reached, it is possible that the estate administrator surrenders the estate into bankruptcy (the Code of Inheritance, Chapter 19, section 12a-b).

225. After the estate has been wound up, the administrator notifies the beneficiaries and prepares a report. Furthermore, once the distribution of the estate has been effected and become legally final, the estate administrator gives each shareholder the property due to him or her (the Inheritance Code, Chapter 19, section 16).

If an executor has been appointed in a will, he/she administers the estate. The scope of the executor's powers depends on the will. In case a will does not stipulate the executor's powers (as is often the case), he/she has the same competence as a court-nominated administrator. An exception to this is that an executor is not entitled

174. *See* European Judicial Network in Civil and Commercial Matters: Succession—Finland, at: e-justice.europa.eu/content_succession-166-fi-en.do?member=1. However, real estate may not be transferred to a third party by the estate administrator without the shareholders' permission (the Code of Inheritance, Ch. 19, s. 14). If the permission cannot be acquired, the court may grant the measure on petition of the administrator.

to surrender the estate into bankruptcy. In addition, a nomination of an executor does not preclude the right of the widow to participate in the administration of the estate (the Inheritance Code, Chapter 19, section 21).

As mentioned earlier, even though an executor is appointed in a will, it is possible to petition for an appointment of an administrator. It is noteworthy, though, that an executor has a right to be nominated as an administrator unless there exist certain special reasons why this should not happen (the Inheritance Code, Chapter 19, section 4).

§4. Control of the Administration

226. There are two categories of the control of the administration. The first one is the control that goes on during the administration. The second category is the control that takes place after the estate has been wound up in full.

If the shareholders have chosen private administration, each of them is entitled to make a petition to the court for an estate administrator. The right of the shareholder is not dependent on whether he/she has reasons for the petition. Instead, the change of the administration model is possible at any time during the administration, except for a case where there is an agreement on joint administration (including an idea that it is left undistributed until further notice or a specified period of time, the Inheritance Code, Chapter 24, section 1).

227. If an administrator has been nominated to wind up and manage the estate, joint administration by the shareholders ceases. However, the shareholders still have certain rights and measures in order to ensure due administration of the estate. Even one of the shareholders or a person whose right is dependent on the winding up the estate, is able to petition the court to order that the administrator have to render an account of the administration. Another option is to appoint a person to audit the administration and prepare report concerning it (the Code of Inheritance, Chapter 19, section 18).

If it turns out that an estate administrator is not suitable for managing the estate, he/she might be dismissed. This is possible on the petition of a person whose right is dependent on the administration (the Code of Inheritance, Chapter 19, section 6). The court may dismiss an administrator even on its own initiative if it learns factors that show an administrator to be unsuitable to continue in his/her task.

228. The control following the settlement of the estate entails provisions according to which compensation for damages is payable. In private administration each shareholder in the estate and in official administration an administrator is obliged to act prudently. Accordingly, if damage is caused to the estate property deliberately or through negligence, one is liable to indemnify for the damage (the Code of Inheritance, Chapter 18, section 19).

Provisions concerning the discharge and liability of an administrator apply correspondingly to the executor of a will (the Code of Inheritance, Chapter 19, section 21).

§5. Distribution of the Estate

229. After the administration of the estate property has been carried out, the next step is its distribution to the heirs (unless otherwise contracted by them according to Chapter 24 of the Inheritance Code).[175] Each shareholder is at this stage entitled to demand a distribution (the Inheritance Code, Chapter 23, section 1). A shareholder is also entitled to prohibit the distribution, if legatees are not yet asserted or debts not paid or the funds needed for their payment not placed into special care (the Inheritance Code, Chapter 23, section 2).

The parties to the estate may decide together how to distribute the estate property between them (a private distribution, the Inheritance Code, Chapter 23, section 3). If the distribution is done by a mutual agreement, a report of the decisions made is drawn up (a distribution deed). The deed has to be signed by the beneficiaries. In addition attestation by two impartial and uninterested witnesses is required (the Inheritance Code, Chapter 23, section 9).[176]

230. Each shareholder is also entitled to demand an official distribution and therefore petition for a court order in where an estate distributor is appointed. The right of a shareholder to decide whether to apply for an official distribution is not dependent on how the estate was administered: privately or officially. In latter cases, though, it is common that the same person is appointed to act both as an administrator and the distributor. According to the Inheritance Code, Chapter 23, section 4, the distributor has to be suitable for the task. In practice the suitability is interpreted to cover both impartiality and expertise in the area of family and inheritance law. In legal literature the distributor has been defined as an extension of a court and therefore the standard of proficiency is set high. Instead, there are no corresponding requirement of impartiality and high professional expertise for the estate administrators. The Inheritance Code, Chapter 19, section 4, reads that the court should appoint as an estate administrator a person who can be presumed capable of settling the estate with the skill demanded by the type of the estate and who accepts the appointment. It follows that even a shareholder may be appointed for the task of an estate administrator (in case there is consensus among other shareholders) whereas a shareholder can never be appointed to act as an estate distributor.

231. The estate distributor must strive to reach an agreement between the heirs. In order to fulfill this obligation, the distributor has to stipulate the time and place where the estate will be distributed, and has to invite all heirs to attend the meeting. If an agreement is reached between all shareholders, the distributor is bound by it and the estate must be distributed accordingly. The agreement binds even in cases where it is only partial, for instance, if it covers only question on the valuation of certain pieces of property belonging to the estate.

175. If a deceased was married, the marital regime is dissolved prior to the distribution of the estate (the Inheritance Code, Ch. 23, s. 1). In case a marital right has been excluded, the property should be separated before the estate property may be distributed to the heirs.

176. If a shareholder of the estate does not have legal capacity or is for other reason represented by a guardian in the distribution, the distribution report needs to be accepted by a guardianship authority (the Guardianship Act, s. 34).

232. If no agreement between the shareholders is reached, the distributor decides how the estate is distributed among the heirs. In this respect, he/she applies provisions of the Inheritance Code. Powers of the distributor include specifying shares of each heir and making a valuation of each piece of property that the estate includes. Thirdly, the distributor has to decide what property each of the heirs receives from the estate. The distributor is tied by a rule that is stipulated in the Inheritance Code, Chapter 23, section 8, which lays down the foundation for the distribution. According to it each shareholder is entitled to "a share of all types of property in the estate." However, an item that cannot suitably be divided into shares or separated can, if possible, be allotted into the same share. In practice the rule is difficult to follow and therefore the distributor may provide the court proof according to which it is obvious that the estate cannot be distributed as specified by the above-mentioned rules. Following the proposal of the distributor, the district court may order that the distributor is entitled to sell an item belonging to the estate, or, if necessary, the order may cover all of the estate property. After the property is sold, the distribution is completed. Selling the estate property is, thus, the last option, an exception to the rule and entitlements for selling objects belonging to the estate property are seldom granted by the courts.

If the distributor is appointed, he/she prepares and signs a distribution deed.[177] The distribution report forms the basis for distributing the estate but as such it does not hold an enforceable title. In other words, enforcement proceedings cannot be initiated on its basis and any enforcement measure requires a separate court order.

233. Beneficiaries are entitled to contest the distribution within six months' time, by bringing proceedings against the other beneficiaries. In official distribution, carried out the court-assigned distributor, it is possible to contest both the material and formal correctness and validity of the distribution. Also the private distribution can be contested in a court, but only on the basis that it was not carried out according to the proper forms (the Inheritance Code, Chapter 23, section 10).

177. If a guardian has entered into an agreement on behalf of a shareholder, the distribution may proceed according to the agreement and the estate distributor is entitled to consider whether the agreement is in the best interests of the ward (the Inheritance Code, Ch. 23, s. 7).

Selected Bibliography

English Material

Eira Kuisma: Comparative Study on Enforcement Procedures of Family Rights. National Report Finland. JLS/C4/2005/06.

Eva Gottberg: Study on Matrimonial Property Regimes and the Property of Unmarried Couples in Private International Law and internal Law. National Report: Finland. Commission Européenne JAI/A3/2001/03. http://ec.europa.eu/civiljustice/publications/docs/regimes/finland_report_en.pdf.

Hilkka Salmenkylä: Finland. In: J. Stewart (ed.): Family Law – Jurisdictional Comparisons 2013. Thomson Reuters 2013 pp. 183–200.

Kirsti Kurki-Suonio: Parental Responsibilities – Finland. Commission on European Family Law: Country Reports. http://ceflonline.net/country-reports-for-finland/.

Kirsti Kurki-Suonio: Property Relationship Between Spouses – Finland. Commission on European Family Law: Country Reports, 2008. http://ceflonline.net/wp-content/uploads/Finland-Property.pdf.

Markku Helin: Finland. In: R. Frimston – A. Ruck Keene – C. Van Overdijk – A.D. Ward (eds.): The International Protection of Adults. Oxford University Press 2015, pp. 356–363.

Matti Savolainen: Grounds for Divorce and Maintenance Between Former Spouses – Finland, 2002. http://ceflonline.net/wp-content/uploads/Finland-Divorce.pdf.

Salla Silvola: Informal Relationships – Finland. Commission on European Family Law: Country Reports, 2015. http://ceflonline.net/country-reports-for-finland/.

Tuulikki Mikkola: The Risks and Opportunities of Foreign Connections in Marriages: the Proprietary Rights of Spouses. In: B. Atkin (ed.): The International Survey of Family Law, 2008 edition. Jordan Publishing 2008, pp. 77–106.

Urpo Kangas: Finlande. http://ec.europa.eu/civiljustice/publications/docs/report_conflits_finland.pdf.

Finnish Material

Ahti Saarenpää: Avioliittolain muutokset. Rovaniemi 1992.

Ahti Saarenpää: Perintö ja jäämistö. Rovaniemi 1994.

Selected Bibliography

Anna Mäki-Petäjä-Leinonen: Ikääntymisen ennakointi. Helsinki 2013.

Anna-Kaisa Aaltonen: Huoltoriitojen sovittelu tuomioistuimessa. Kauppakamari 2015.

Antti Kolehmainen – Timo Räbinä: Jäämistösuunnittelu. Helsinki 2012.

Aulis Aarnio – Markku Helin: Suomen avioliitto-oikeus, Helsinki 1992.

Aulis Aarnio – Urpo Kangas: Perhevarallisuusoikeus. Helsinki 2010.

Eva Gottberg: Perhesuhteet ja lainsäädäntö. Turku 2013.

Johanna Tornberg – Matti Kuuliala: Suomen edunvalvontaoikeus. Helsinki 2015.

Markku Helin & Tuula Linna & Matti Rintala: Huolto- ja tapaamispäätöksen täytäntöönpano. Helsinki 1997.

Markku Helin: Isyyslaki. Helsinki 2016.

Pekka Tuunainen: Perintö, testamentti ja velka. Helsinki 2015.

Pertti Välimäki: Edunvalvontaoikeus. Sanoma Pro 2013.

Pertti Välimäki: Osituksen sovittelu avioeroon perustuvassa toimitusosituksessa. Helsinki 1995.

Sanna Koulu: Lapsen huolto- ja tapaamissopimukset. Kauppakamari 2014.

Suvianna Hakalehto-Wainio & Liisa Nieminen (toim./eds.): Lapsioikeus murroksessa. Helsinki 2013.

Tapani Lohi: Aviovarallisuusoikeus. Helsinki 2016.

Tapani Lohi: Ennakkoperinnöstä. Helsinki 1999.

Tapani Lohi: Ositus, tasinko ja sivullissuoja. Jyväskylä 2013.

Tuomo Antila: Edunvalvontavaltuutus. Vantaa 2007.

Tuulikki Mikkola: Lesken asema jäämistö- ja vero-oikeudessa. Juva 2010.

Tuulikki Mikkola: Yhteisomistus. Helsinki 2017.

Index

The numbers here refer to paragraph numbers.

Index

Index

Made in the USA
Monee, IL
16 September 2026

63296749R00070